HOW TO
BEAT YOUR
CHESS
COMPUTER

Batsford Chess Library

HOW TO BEAT YOUR CHESS COMPUTER

RAYMOND KEENE
and
DAVID LEVY

An Owl Book
Henry Holt and Company
New York

First published in the United States in 1992 by
Henry Holt and Company, Inc., 115 West 18th Street,
New York, New York 10011.
Originally published in Great Britain in 1991
by B. T. Batsford Ltd.

Library of Congress Catalog Card Number: 92-52734

ISBN 0-8050-2316-X (An Owl Book: pbk.)

Henry Holt books are available at special discounts
for bulk purchases for sales promotions, premiums,
fund-raising, or educational use. Special editions
or book excerpts can also be created to specification.

For details contact: Special Sales Director,
Henry Holt and Company, Inc., 115 West 18th Street,
New York, New York 10011.

First American Edition—1992

Printed in the United Kingdom
Recognizing the importance of preserving
the written word, Henry Holt and Company, Inc.,
by policy, prints all of its first editions
on acid-free paper.∞

10 9 8 7 6 5 4 3 2 1

Advisor: R.D. Keene GM, OBE
Technical Editor: Andrew Kinsman

Contents

Preface

Chess playing computer programs have made great strides during the past few years. Nowadays it is commonplace for programs to distinguish themselves in matches or tournaments with human opponents. The most notable successes have been those of the American program DEEP THOUGHT which, in 1988, tied for first place in a tournament ahead of a number of Masters, Grandmasters and even one former World Champion (Mikhail Tal)! DEEP THOUGHT has defeated various Grandmasters: Bent Larsen, Tony Miles, Robert Byrne. It has also crushed one of the authors of this book, David Levy, who had hitherto been able to succeed with his own brand of computer hostile play against all comers. Levy lost a match against DEEP THOUGHT by a score of 4–0 in December 1989, thereby ending an era during which most chess masters had not taken programs at all seriously.

At the time of writing, Gary Kasparov has stated that he considers his mission in life to be the successful defence of mankind against DEEP THOUGHT and its successors.

You, the reader of this book, will probably not have the opportunity to play against DEEP THOUGHT, but there is an enormous range of commercially available chess software to choose from. Many chess enthusiasts now own chess computers or chess playing programs for their home computers. This applies to players of almost all strengths — even some masters. Playing regularly against a computer program is an ideal way of improving your own chess ability. Commercially available chess programs and chess computers usually have a number of different skill levels, and by playing on a level which is roughly commensurate with your own ability you will be able to monitor your progress as you gradually overtake the computer. Once you are able to beat it regularly on one particular level, set it on the next highest level and play until you are also able to defeat it regularly on the new level. And so on.

If you have been careful in your choice of chess computer, some of the higher levels will be too difficult for you. The purpose of this book is to give you enough extra understanding so that you will eventually be able to defeat your chess computer no matter on which level it is set. Does this mean that eventually you will have no further use for your computer? Far from it! This book also explains how you can use your chess computer as an analysis partner to suggest and test out new ideas for you in the opening.

For those interested in who wrote which chapter David Levy wrote chapters 1, 2, 3, 4, 10 and the appendix, and Raymond Keene wrote chapters 5, 6, 7, 8, and 9. The appendix first appeared in *The Chess Computer Handbook* (Batsford, 1984).

In writing this book we have aimed to provide information which will be both useful and entertaining. We hope that it will help you to get more enjoyment from playing your electronic opponent.

Ray Keene, David Levy
London, May 1991

1 The Openings

Your chess computer has been programmed with a number of "book" openings variations. These variations will have been selected from established opening theory, and may have been copied from one or more books on the openings. If the number of moves in your program's openings book is small, the chances are high that all the variations will be well known main lines. But you may have a computer with a large openings book, in which case from time to time you can expect the computer to play an obscure or even unsound variation against you.

You can keep track of your computer's opening preferences, just as you would in a match against a known human opponent. This will help you to prepare for your games against the computer. As you play more and more games you will learn more and more about precisely which variations and sub-variations your computer plays. This will enable you to study your own openings books, or to look up analyses of specific variations which you may have found in chess magazines. Eventually you will probably know enough about your opponent's built-in openings repertoire to be able to side-track the computer into lines that you have studied thoroughly. You will then be able to play confidently in the opening, and usually you will secure an advantage in the opening simply by knowing more than your opponent about the book lines that it plays. Remember — the computer's openings book is fixed in tablets of silicon, whereas you are free to take a book off the shelf whenever you wish and enrich your knowledge of any specific opening or variation.

One idea which might occur to you is to see whether your computer will fall into a standard openings trap. This is very unlikely. The computer's openings book will almost certainly avoid such traps, and if the computer gets taken out of its openings book before it gets to the critical position just before your trap will be set, it is most likely to see what you have in mind. This is because the computer's strongest point is its tactical ability.

Here is an example. In the Sicilian Defence, after the moves **1 e4 c5 2 ♘f3 ♘c6 3 d4 cxd4 4 ♘xd4 g6 5 ♘c3 ♗g7 6 ♗e3 ♘f6 7 ♗c4 0–0 8 ♗b3 ♘a5 9 e5**

Would you expect the computer, as Black, to fall into the famous Fischer–Reshevsky trap and play 9 ... ♘e8? The answer should be "no", unless your computer is set on a fairly low level. The reason is that if this position is still in its openings book the move 9 ... ♘e8 will certainly not be played, and if the program is out of book it will probably find: 10 ♗xf7+! ♔xf7 (or 10 ... ♖xf7 11 ♘e6, winning the queen) 11 ♘e6! ♔xe6 12 ♕d5+ ♔f5 13 e6+ ♔g4 (or 13 ... ♔f6 14 ♗d4 mate) 14 ♕g5 mate. The sequence beginning with 9 ... ♘e8 and ending with White's 14th move is 10-ply (half-moves) deep, but all the moves from 10 ♗xf7+ onwards are checks or replies to check, which means that the computer will probably see the whole variation in its tactical look-ahead. You should always remember that although your computer may be looking "only" 5, 6 or 7 ply ahead in most variations, it probably extends its search to greater depths for tactical variations (those that contain only checks, replies to check and captures). So playing for openings traps will probably not work if your computer is set to respond within (say) 2 minutes per move or longer. In fact, some of the better chess computers would see the above variation when thinking for only a few seconds!

How else, apart from knowing more "book" variations than your opponent, can you hope to gain the upper hand against your computer in the opening? The answer lies in gaining an insight into how your computer's "evaluation function" works.

The evaluation function is the part of the program that tells the computer how good or bad its position appears to be. Each time the computer reaches the end of a variation in its analysis, it calls the evaluation function and asks "What is the score for this position?" It then compares this score with the scores for the other positions it has found at the end of a line of analysis, and chooses the move which maximizes its score.

The most important feature in a program's evaluation function is, naturally, material. This means that you can nearly always count on your computer grabbing, and trying to hold on to, any material that is on offer. Computers are the greediest chess players around! Show a computer a pawn and it will snap it up. This greed will often give rise to opportunities for you, since you know that your opponent is going to take the bait unless it can see a clear refutation. Here is a well known example which could be used on almost all of the first generation of chess computers in the late 1970s: **1 d4 d5 2 c4 dxc4 3 e3** (threatening to win back the pawn) **3 ... b5** (hanging on to it) **4 a4** (threatening to win back the pawn) **4 ... c6** (hanging on to it) **5 axb5**. If now 5 ... cxb5, White wins material with 6 ♕f3. Of course you would not expect this idea to work against one of today's chess computers in the intermediate to strong range. These computers would not have the move 3 ... b5 in their openings books and would not be likely to play it after analyzing to a depth of 5 ply, since their tactical search would probably find the refutation. But there are still some of the inexpensive beginners' machines which will fall foul of this trick.

You can try to take advantage of your computer's inability to generalize by creating a position similar to the one arising after 1 d4 d5 2 c4 dxc4 3 e3, but where the computer is already out of its openings book. This will be made much easier for you if you know the program's depth of search. You can then play the move e3 in a position in which the key move ♕f3 (winning material by attacking the a8 rook) is just over its "horizon". As an extreme example, let us suppose that the computer's search depth is only 1-ply with no extra tactical look-ahead. After the move 3 e3 the computer will happily play 3 ... b5 because it can see no threat — everything is defended!

Since material is by far the most significant feature in evaluation functions, it is the easiest one to use as bait. But when you have played a lot of games against your chess computer you will have learned some of its other rigid ideas. Not only will all chess computers grab material and hang on for dear life, most of them will make other decisions based on the information embedded in the most important features in their evaluation functions. Possibly the best example of this is the type of position that arises in the Sicilian Defence, when White has a knight on d4 and Black has a knight on c6. The move ♘d4xc6 is known to be (nearly always) bad for White, because by recapturing with the b-pawn Black strengthens his centre and is better prepared for the thematic thrust ... d5. In addition, it will often be possible for Black to create queenside counterplay by putting a rook on the semi-open b-file.

But computers think differently from humans. Let us look at a concrete example:

1 e4 c5 2 ♘f3 ♘c6 3 d4 cxd4 4 ♘xd4 e6

In this position, if the computer was already out of its openings book, its thinking would go something like this: "If I play 5 ♘xc6 he can recapture with the d-pawn or the b-pawn. If he recaptures with the d-pawn I can play 6 ♕xd8+, depriving him of castling rights. If he recaptures with the b-pawn he has an isolated a-pawn. Isolated pawns are weak." (The computer represents the weakness of isolated pawns by deducting a penalty within the evaluation function for every isolated pawn.)

The above reasoning leads the computer to conclude that ♘xc6 is a good move. The human player as Black would rejoice at having a half-open b-file and a strong pawn centre. This is an example, in which the computer is at fault, of what Botvinnik once described as a chess player's greatest art — the ability to create positions in which the normal relative values cease to exist. Normally isolated pawns are weak. Here the weakness of Black's isolated a-pawn is not significant when compared to the other factors.

I have often taken advantage of this particular defect in computers' thinking. It is worth studying the following games because even in the early 1990s chess computers seem still to believe that ♘xc6 is usually a good move.

CHESS 4.5–David Levy
Pittsburgh, 1977

1 e4 c5 2 ♘f3 d6 3 d4 cxd4 4 ♘xd4 ♘f6 5 ♘c3 g6 6 f3 ♗g7 7 ♗e3 0–0 8 ♕d2 ♘c6 9 ♗c4

In a couple of blitz games against the same opponent I had faced the alternative 9 0–0–0. My reply had been 9 ... a6, to take the program out of book, and after the inevitable 10 ♘xc6 bxc6 I won both games with attacks along the b-file!

9 ... a6

This is bad (too slow) against humans, but I fully expected my opponent to isolate my a-pawn.

10 ♘xc6 bxc6 11 0–0 ♘d7 12 f4 ♘b6 13 ♗e2 ♗e6 14 b3?

Preventing ... ♘c4, but at the cost of weakening the queenside.

14 ... ♘c8 15 a3 ♕a5 16 b4 ♕c7 17 f5 ♗d7 18 ♗h6

Correct is 18 ♔h1, followed by ♖f3, ♗h6 and ♖h3. But my opponent did not understand how to build up the attack.

18 ... ♕b6+ 19 ♔h1 ♕d4! 20 ♕xd4 ♗xd4 21 ♖f3

If 21 ♗xf8, then ♗xc3 22 ♗h6 ♗xa1 23 ♖xa1 gxf5, winning a pawn.

21 ... ♗g7 22 ♗xg7 ♔xg7 23 ♖b1 ♘b6 24 ♖3f1 ♖fb8 25 ♖bd1 f6 26 a4? a5 27 b5 cxb5 28 axb5 ♖c8 29 ♖d3 ♖c5 30 ♖g3 ♖8c8 31 ♖1f3 a4 32 h4

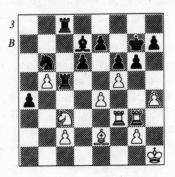

At this point in the game CHESS 4.5 still considered itself to be ahead by half a pawn, the result of the isolated pawn penalty! Of course, Black is winning.

32 ... a3 33 fxg6

Here the program realised that it was doing badly.

33 ... hxg6 34 ♖e3 ♗e6 35 h5 g5 36 ♘d5 a2 37 ♖a3 ♗xd5 38 exd5 ♖xc2 39 ♗d1 ♖d2 40 ♔h2 ♖c1 41 ♗b3 a1(♛) 42 ♖xa1 ♖xa1 0-1

CHESS 4.7–David Levy
Toronto, 1978

1 ♘c3 c5 2 e4 ♘c6 3 f4 a6 4 ♘f3 g6 5 d4 cxd4 6 ♘xd4 ♗g7 7 ♗e3 d6 8 ♘xc6? bxc6 9 ♗e2 ♖b8 10 ♛c1

Already White is on the defensive as a result of the half-open b-file.

10 ... ♛a5 11 ♗d2 ♛b6 12 ♘a4 ♛a7 13 ♘c3 ♗d4 14 ♘d1 ♘f6 15 c3 ♗b6 16 ♛c2 ♘g4 17 ♛a4 0-0 18 ♗xg4 ♗xg4 19 ♛xc6 ♗xd1 20 ♔xd1 ♗e3, and with White's king stuck in the centre the game was an easy win for Black.

David Levy–CHESS 4.7
Toronto, 1978

1 c4 ♘f6 2 a3 ♘c6 3 ♘c3 d5 4 cxd5 ♘xd5 5 d3

In order to encourage:

5 ... ♘xc3 6 bxc3 e5

So now I have a Sicilian, with the advantage of an extra tempo as well as the better pawn centre.

7 g3 ♗e7 8 ♗g2 ♛d6 9 ♘f3 ♗e6 10 0-0 0-0 11 ♛a4 ♛c5 12 ♗d2 b5? 13 ♛c2 f6 14 ♖fb1 ♖ad8 15 ♛b2 ♖b8 16 ♗e3 ♛d6 17 ♘d2

The knight is heading for b3 or e4, followed by ♘c5 or ♗c5.
17 ... ♗d5 18 ♗xd5+ ♛xd5 19 ♕b3 ♛xb3 20 ♘xb3 f5 21 ♗c5 ♗d6 22 ♖b2 ♔h8 23 ♖ab1 a6 24 ♗xd6 cxd6 25 ♘d2 f4 26 ♔g2 fxg3 27 hxg3 ♖ad8 28 a4! ♘a7!

Since 28 ... bxa4 29 ♖b6 would be extremely unpleasant for Black.
29 ♘e4 bxa4 30 ♖b6 d5 31 ♘c5 ♘b5 32 ♘xa4 ♖a8 33 c4 dxc4 34 dxc4 ♘d4 35 e3 ♘f3 36 c5 ♘g5 37 c6 ♘e4 38 c7 ♖xf2+ 39 ♔g1 ♖ff8 40 ♖b8 h5 41 ♖xa8 ♖xa8 42 ♖b8+ ♔h7 and Black resigned.

Another way to take advantage of a chess computer's evaluation function is to offer it the opportunity to double your pawns in a position in which the doubled pawns are of little or no consequence. Just as your opponent will rub its circuits together with glee at the prospect of saddling you with an isolated pawn, it will be almost as happy, if not happier, to double your pawns. Try the following idea if you get the chance:

YOU–COMPUTER

1 e4 g6 2 ♘c3 ♗g7 3 d3

Most chess computers are told that bishops and knights are of equal value. Some are told that bishops are very slightly better than knights (perhaps 3.2 pawns instead of 3.0 for the knight). But very few understand that this difference is rarely small enough to warrant giving up a fianchettoed bishop for a knight, merely so as to double the human player's pawns. Here, since your computer will already be out of its openings book, it will be thinking: "Oh good. I can double his pawns." The result will be **3 ... ♗xc3+** which leaves Black with gaping weaknesses on the dark squares around his king after he castles kingside. You and I know that one does not lightly give up a fianchettoed king's bishop for a knight, but most computer programs lack this information. After 3 ... ♗xc3+ 4 bxc3, White stands clearly better.

Another example is the Accelerated Dragon in the Sicilian Defence. If you are White and your game opens: **1 e4 c5 2 ♘f3 ♘c6 3 d4 cxd4 4 ♘xd4 g6 5 ♘c3 ♗g7**, why not try **6 ♘f3?!** Your opponent will now get a surge of electrons as it exclaims: "What a moron this guy is. I can saddle him with doubled, isolated pawns. Off with its head." The computer proudly announces 6 ... ♗xc3+ and after 7 bxc3 you calmly develop your pieces and eventually build up a mating attack against its king on g8, by capitalizing on the weak dark squares near its king (f6, g7, h6).

This theme of gaining the two bishops can also occur in a different guise. After 1 e4, you could play, as Black, 1 ... ♘a6. The idea is simply to goad your opponent into playing 2 ♗xa6 so as to leave you with doubled, isolated a-pawns. In fact, Black's play along the b-file and the advantage of two bishops for bishop and knight provide more than enough compensation for the doubling and isolation of the a-pawns. Should White not play 2 ♗xa6 you can play 2 ... b6 followed by ... c5, or you can leave your b-pawn on b7 and wait for a few more moves, to give White the chance to play ♗xa6 at a later stage.

This same idea can be put into operation on the kingside. For example (you are Black): **1 d4 ♘h6 2 ♗xh6 gxh6**. Now you have doubled, isolated h-pawns, but you also have the bishop pair and the half-open g-file. Assume that the computer will plan on castling kingside so you plan to castle on the opposite wing and launch an attack along the g-file: ... b6, ... ♗b7, ... ♘c6, ... e6, ... ♕ moves, ... 0-0-0, ... ♗d6, ... ♖dg8, ... ♖g7, ... ♖hg8, etc. You can improvise all sorts of interesting ideas based on the theme: The monster likes me to have doubled and/or isolated pawns.

Here is an example from the Modern Defence which illustrates the point rather well. **1 e4 g6 2 d4 ♗g7 3 c4 d6 4 ♘c3 ♘c6 5 d5**

If the computer does not have this position in its openings book it would be quite likely to make the serious strategic error of trading on c3: **5 ... ♗xc3+ 6 bxc3**. Now White's c-pawns are doubled. So, as in the Accelerated Dragon example above, the computer would be quite happy with Black's position while you would be delighted to attack on the kingside and take advantage of the dark squared weaknesses on g7, h6 and f6.

Another common failing in computer programs' understanding of opening principles is the way that they will blindly develop their knights on f3 (f6) and c3 (c6) once they are out of book, unless they can see a very good reason not to. The reason is that, once out of book, programs tend to use their middlegame evaluation function as the basis for making all decisions. If the game is still in the opening phase this means that the program is using the wrong principles, and you can take advantage of your program's inability to understand the principles of good opening play.

The most common appearance of this particular fault is in the queen's pawn openings. In most queen's pawn openings Black strives to play the move ... c5 at some stage or other, and for this reason the development of Black's b8 knight is usually delayed until after ... c5 has been played, or else the knight is developed to d7 in order to support the thrust ... c5. If you kick a program out of the book, it immediately concludes that its b8 knight belongs on c6, because from c6 the knight exerts more influence on the centre (attacking e5 and d4) than it does from d7. Furthermore, the program knows that the development of its minor pieces should be completed as quickly as possible, and so it will want to bring out this knight. Examples of this failing can be seen in the HITECH v DEEP THOUGHT game on page 43, and Dominic Lawson v DEEP THOUGHT on page 33.

Finally, let us consider a more general point on the subject of the opening inadequacies of computer programs. Every chess opening or variation has at least one theme. For example, in the French Defence Black normally tries to advance his c-pawn to c5 as soon as possible, in order to undermine White's pawn centre. If your computer is out of book, it will almost certainly not know what thematic moves to aim for, and it may not find the right idea in the position. This means that your computer will be playing without an understanding of the correct strategy in that particular type of position, whereas you will know the correct strategy. As an example, look at the opening of a game I played against DEEP THOUGHT. I was White and the game began: **1 d4 f5 2 ♗g5 h6 3 ♗h4 g5 4 e3 ♘f6 5 ♗g3 d6 6 c3 ♗g7 7 ♘d2 0–0 8 f3!? ♘c6**

Probably the knight should not be developed here, since Black may want to play ... c6 at a later stage.

9 ♗c4+

This move was played to encourage ... d5, which I had felt was the most likely reply to come from a program. In fact the square e5 is crucial in the Dutch Defence, so Black should move its king in this position, leaving the d6 pawn to exert control over e5.

9 ... d5

After this move I should have played 10 ♗b5, followed by ♗xc6, and then White could build up pressure based partly on his domination of the e5 square. This would have been the logical way to capitalize on the feeble strategy of ... ♘c6 and ... d5.

Summary

Let us now summarize how you can best take advantage of your computer in the opening:

(1) Your computer probably does not understand very much, if anything, about the *principles* of openings play. Therefore, if you take it out of its openings book while the game is still in the opening phase, it will be playing in accordance with its middlegame principles and will probably make strategic errors early on.

(2) Try to create positions in which your computer can give up a good bishop for a knight, in return for doubling and/or isolating your pawns.

(3) Try to identify the idiosyncrasies of your computer's middlegame play. You will then be able to take it out of book in a position where you have a reasonable expectation of it making stereotyped moves which are wrong for that particular type of position.

(4) Learn more about some of the variations that the computer plays, so that you can take advantage of its fixed openings knowledge.

2 The Middlegame

Trying to Win with a Combination

Every chess player loves to win a game with a pretty combination. Playing for combinative possibilities is a viable idea when your opponent is human because human players are wont to overlook tactical ideas from time to time. They simply do not notice the idea until it is too late. Computer programs do not "overlook" tactics in the same way that humans do. A human player might miss a 3-ply combination because he simply did not consider the first move of the combination, for example a non-capturing move which puts the queen en prise. If a program does not see a combination it is solely because the combination is too deep for its search algorithm, not because it overlooked the move that starts the combination. For this reason you should be careful not think: "If I play ♖e1 and it does not see my threat, I have a 3-move combination to win a pawn." Forget it. Your computer will almost certainly see the 3-move combination unless it is a beginner's machine set on a low level.

The fact that you should not be trying to win by combinative means should not blunt your alertness to combinative possibilities. The crucial issue is that your combinative ideas should be by-products of your strategic planning. There is no harm in making a good strategic move if it also threatens to play a combination, in fact your threat may make it more difficult for the computer to counter your strategic idea. If you are able to play a successful combination it will almost certainly be due to one of two factors:

(a) *Your combination is too deep for the computer*. If you can find such a combination you should be proud of yourself, because your computer thinks more deeply in tactical positions than it does in quiet positions. You can expect the computer to conduct a "full-width" search in which it examines every move at every depth, and then to extend this search in variations involving captures, checks and, possibly, direct threats. The depth of its full-width search is sometimes easy to see — some chess computers display the current depth of their full-width search. You can then be certain that the computer will spot any combination whose conclusion lies within this search depth.

If, for example, your computer is set to a level on which its full-width search is always 5-ply or more, then if you think you have seen a 3-ply combination to win a bishop you can be certain that you are wrong! Re-examine your analysis and you will work out why this is, and this will help you to gain a better insight into the tactical possibilities in the position. An analogous situation once arose in a game between Tal and Korchnoi. Tal thought for a long time and offered a pawn sacrifice. Korchnoi replied quickly, refusing the pawn. After the game Tal asked Korchnoi whether he had analyzed the acceptance of the sacrifice, to be told "No. I trusted you"! In the same way you should trust your computer to see everything within its full-width search depth. In addition, if a combination starts within this search depth or immediately after it, the computer's analytical powers can extend for several more ply. So if the computer's full-width search depth is 5-ply, when making your move you should expect the computer to spot combinations for both players which commence within 6-ply of the current position:

1st ply: Your move

2nd ply: Computer's 1st ply move when considering its reply.

3rd ply: Your move (computer's 2nd ply)

4th ply: Computer's move (its 3rd ply)

5th ply: Your move (computer's 4th ply)

6th ply: Computer's move (its 5th ply). If this move or the next move is the first move of the combination, or if the combination started at an earlier ply, then you should expect the program to spot it, unless the conclusion of the combination is too deep for the computer's extended search.

It is often difficult to know just how deeply your computer can search in a combinative variation. The instruction manual may tell you — it may indicate the maximum depth of search for a given level. But since this part of the search is highly selective, you cannot be sure about which moves the computer will examine and which it will reject.

In summary, be careful! Have more faith in a combination that has arisen as the end result of a successful strategy than a combination which you think (but are not certain) may be beyond the computer's search horizon. And finally, always be on the lookout for possible combinations by the computer. If there is a way to win material or force checkmate within the computer's search depth it should always spot it.

(b) *Your combination could not be prevented by the time the computer spotted it.* This type of combination often arises when you have been building up pressure and the computer has been steadily defending. Eventually you may reach a position where the computer sees that you can gain a massive positional advantage, and the only thing it can do to stop you allows you to win material with a combination. For example, the game might be a positional struggle which revolves around the question of whether or not you can infiltrate your queen to be near your opponent's king. If most of the moves are non-tactical, in other words they are not captures or checks, the computer will not have any reason to extend its search depth to the point where it would spot a deeply rooted combination. Suddenly the computer sees that 5-ply later you might have your queen and some other pieces poised near its king. The king safety and king attack features in its evaluation function might add up to (say) a 2 pawn disadvantage for the computer in that particular variation, so it would then be willing to concede a pawn in order to stave off an even more serious loss. The computer would sacrifice 1 pawn in order to avoid suffering a positional loss equivalent, in its evaluation function, to 2 pawns. This desire by the computer to avoid some observable loss within its search horizon can sometimes lead to even bigger gains for you, due to a factor called the "Horizon Effect".

The Horizon Effect

The syndrome known as the Horizon Effect manifests itself in positions in which a program cannot see some crucial move because that move is beyond the horizon of its look-ahead analysis. As a result of this short sightedness, the program makes a serious error. A simple example will help to explain this phenomenon (see diagram 6 overleaf).

It is Black to move, and although White is a long way behind in material, Black must cede most of the extra material because of events on the a1–h8 long diagonal: the black queen is lost to the white bishop. Let us assume that Black is conducting a full width search to a depth

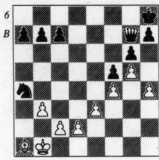

of 2-ply and then evaluating all positions at that depth. What Black sees
and thinks can be summarised by the following table:

Black's 1st ply move:	♘a4–b2	♘a4–c3+	Any other
White's 2nd ply move:	♗a1xb2	♗a1xc3	Capture Black's queen
Net material loss:	3 pawns	3 pawns	At least 5.7 pawns

It is quite clear from the above table that Black does much better to
play its knight from a4 to either b2 or c3, because that will lose only 3
pawns worth of material, whereas any other move will lose at least 5.7
pawns (we are employing 3.3 pawns as the value of a bishop). Yet a
human chess player can easily see that after the knight is captured,
White will still go on to win the black queen, because nothing important
has changed along the a1–h8 diagonal. The essential features concerning
that diagonal, which appear in the above position, still exist. What the
program has done, in playing ♘a4–b2 or ♘a4–c3+, is to push the loss of
the queen for bishop over its horizon, so that it can no longer see the
loss as being inevitable. Only after the bishop has captured the knight
will Black realise that it is still faced with the loss of the queen.

This example was bad enough for Black, but in order to show the
sort of thing that has occurred more than once in computer chess
tournaments, we now give a slightly modified example to illustrate the
Horizon Effect at its worst (see diagram 7 overleaf).

Here Black must again lose its queen for the white bishop on a1, but
Black is so much ahead in material that the game will still be an easy
win for Black. But if Black can see only 2-ply ahead, how will be game
continue?

1 ... ♘b2

This is just as good as 1 ... ♘c3+, both of which lose only 3 pawns worth of material, whereas 1 ... ♗d4 loses 3.3 pawns, 1 ... ♖e5 and 1 ... ♖f6 each lose 5 pawns, while other moves lose at least 5.7 pawns.

2 ♗xb2 ♗d4

This loses only 3.3 pawns worth, and is therefore superior to 2 ... ♖e5 and 2 ... ♗f6, each of which loses 5, and to other moves which lose at least 5.7.

3 ♗xd4 ♖e5

I have taken the liberty of assuming that the f8 rook has a greater positional value than its partner on e8, since its greater proximity to the black king gives it more king safety points. The program therefore prefers to give up the e8 rook to losing the f8 rook, and we must not forget that either of these possibilities is seen to be preferable to losing the queen.

4 ♗xe5 ♖f6

Obviously the best move, since anything else loses the queen at once.

5 ♗xf6

So on each of the four previous moves Black has found a way to minimise its material loss, but in so doing it merely pushed a greater disaster over the horizon each time. Now, having given up two minor pieces and two rooks, Black must still lose its queen and White will win the game.

Trying to Win with a Sacrifice

The word "sacrifice" is used here to describe moves which are not part of a combination. Instead we use the term to denote the long term sacrifice of material in return for an important strategic advantage. The game between CRAY BLITZ and David Levy on page 56 is a good example. Examine the position after Black's 19th move. The computer wanted my a-pawn and I was happy to oblige, because in going after this pawn it left itself vulnerable on the kingside. This is typical of the type of sacrifice which is likely to work well against a computer. You can always feel confident when preparing an attack against its king if the program can be distracted, preferably on the opposite wing, by the desire to win material. So long as the culmination of your attack is many moves away, as mine was in the CRAY BLITZ game, the computer will think like this: "I can grab a pawn. He can get some compensation by attacking my king but there is no win for him within my search horizon, therefore there is no win for him. Therefore he does not have enough compensation for the sacrificed pawn. Therefore I shall take it."

Here is another example of a material sacrifice which is made in return for long-range goals. Diagram nine was reached in a game between DEEP THOUGHT (White) and Grandmaster Walter Browne (Black) at the tournament in Long Beach, California, October 1988. It was in this tournament that DEEP THOUGHT defeated the Danish Grandmaster Bent Larsen and tied for first place with Tony Miles, ahead of former World Champion Mikhail Tal. Its loss to Browne was its only defeat in the whole event, and the following year it defeated Tony Miles in an exhibition play-off game.

DEEP THOUGHT–Browne
Long Beach, California 1988

DEEP THOUGHT has just played 21 ♗c2–a4, attacking the black rook on e8. Browne could neutralize this threat with 21 ... ♗c6, but

instead decides on an exchange sacrifice:

21 ... ♛d5!

Now the most solid defensive move is 22 ♝d1, guarding f3, when White stands worse but may be able to stave off the attack against his king. But no self-respecting computer program would resist the temptation to grab the exchange.

22 ♝xe8 ♜xe8 23 ♔g2 ♞c4 24 ♝c1 g5! 25 h3 h5 26 g4 e5 27 ♛d1 f5

"There is too much wood on the fire — enough to melt metal and silicon" — Browne.

28 gxf5 g4 29 hxg4 fxg4 30 ♔g1 ♛xf3 31 ♛xf3 ♝xf3 32 ♝h6 ♔h7 33 ♝d2 ♜f8 34 ♜xe5 ♞xe5 35 ♞e1 ♞c6 0-1

Browne's sacrificial idea is an excellent illustration of the difference between the computer's ability to assess positions and a Grandmaster's ability to assess the same positions. So far as the computer is concerned, if there is no visible compensation for the sacrificed material, the sacrifice must be unsound. In other words, the program's evaluation will give more points to White's extra material than it does to Black's pressure along the a8–h1 diagonal. The Grandmaster concludes that Black will "eventually" be able to capitalize on this pressure. In games against your chess computer you should be on the lookout for situations where you can acquire some sort of long-term pressure or where you can create long-term strategic weaknesses in the computer's position. Remember, the somewhat vague word "eventually" has no place in the computer's precise way of thinking. If you need to sacrifice a little material to achieve this goal, be optimistic!

Avoiding Unnecessary Tactics

It is well known that most computer programs excel at tactics. The reasons have been explained above in the section on "Trying to win with a combination". Unless tactics are also your forte and you feel extremely confident challenging the computer on its home ground, you would be well advised to avoid tactics unless they are an essential ingredient of your game.

Try instead to build up pressure slowly. If you make a move which carries a shallow threat the computer will almost certainly spot the threat and react to it. But if you make a move which threatens to threaten something, or which threatens to threaten to threaten something, there is less chance of the computer detecting what you are up to. The deeper your strategy the better your chances of success.

The following game shows how it is possible to plan a very slow build-up against a computer opponent. This was the final game of my match in 1978, when I won a famous bet. My opponent was the reigning World Computer Champion program, running on a Control Data Corporation Cyber computer.

David Levy–CHESS 4.7
Toronto, 1978

1 c4 ♘f6 2 a3 c6 3 d3 d5 4 ♕c2

A crazy looking move, but there was a good reason. I had observed the program playing the following opening, as White, against Stean one year earlier: 1 e4 b6 2 d4 ♗b7 3 ♘c3 c5 4 dxc5?!, and felt that if the computer wanted to exchange a centre pawn for my wing pawn, why should I stop it?

4 ... dxc4 5 ♕xc4 e5

And so I have a Sicilian formation with colours reversed.

6 ♘f3 ♗d6 7 g3 ♗e6 8 ♕c2 ♘bd7 9 ♗g2 0–0 10 0–0 ♕b6 11 ♘bd2 ♕c5 12 ♕b1

Keeping queens on the board helps maximize the number of legal moves at both players' disposal, and hence reduces the program's maximum search depth. This is because the amount of time that the computer needs to search to any given depth depends on the average number of moves that it needs to consider at each ply. The more moves there are the more time the program will take at that ply, and the less time it will have for the analysis of subsequent plies. For this reason I usually tried to keep queens on until I could create a highly favourable endgame.

12 ... h6 13 b4 ♛b5 14 ♛c2 ♞b6 15 ♗b2 a5 16 a4 ♛a6 17 bxa5 ♛xa5 18 ♗c3 ♛c5 19 ♖fc1 ♞bd7 20 a5 ♛a7 21 ♛b2 ♞g4 22 ♞e4 ♗c7 23 h3 f5 24 hxg4 fxe4 25 dxe4 ♗xg4 26 ♗e1

This overprotecting move is unnecessarily slow. More incisive is 26 ♖cb1. But in any event Black cannot easily prevent White's plan.

26 ... ♞c5 27 ♖cb1 ♖ae8 28 ♗d2

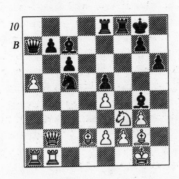

The idea is to put pressure on the knight that protects b7.

28 ... ♖f7 29 ♗e3 ♗d6 30 ♛c2 ♗xf3 31 ♗xf3 ♖a8 32 ♖c1 b6 33 ♔g2 ♛b7 34 axb6 ♖xa1 35 ♖xa1 ♞e6 36 ♖a7 ♛c8 37 ♛a2 ♖f6 38 ♖a8 ♗b8 39 ♗g4 ♔f7 40 ♛a7+ ♗xa7 41 ♖xc8 ♗xb6 42 ♗xe6+ ♖xe6 43 ♗xb6 Black Resigns

Castling on Opposite Wings

This piece of advice applies to the opening as much as to the early middlegame. If you like to attack your opponent's king, try to create positions in which your computer castles before you do and then you castle on the opposite wing. You will probably understand more than the computer does about how to launch a pawn storm against your opponent's king — this is because such attacks frequently require long term sacrifices of a pawn or two in order to open up lines against the enemy king, and long term sacrifices are "unsound" to the computer's way of thinking.

One way you can achieve this goal is by playing opening variations where the players normally castle on opposite wings, such as the Sämisch Variation of the King's Indian Defence or the Yugoslav Attack against the Dragon Variation of the Sicilian. But in most openings the players castle on the same wing (the king side), so some improvisation is needed to achieve your goal. Try experimenting with ideas for developing your minor pieces and your queen, while maintaining a sound pawn structure on the queen side. As soon as the computer castles king side you should prepare for castling on the opposite wing and then you will be ready to launch your attack.

Summary

(1)   Avoid unnecessary tactics.
(2)   Try for a slow, steady build-up.
(3)   Be on the lookout for ways to distract the computer while you launch an attack against its king. The best way to do this is to offer it a chance to grab material, particularly if in doing so it has to put one or more of its pieces out of play. If you enjoy an attacking game, try to castle on the opposite wing from the computer and then attack its king vigorously with your pawns.

3 The Endgame

"Everyone knows that computers cannot play endgames." This was standard advice at the beginning of the 1980s, or even in the mid-1980s, but things have changed. Nevertheless, it remains true that in many endgames the difference in playing ability between yourself and your computer program moves more in your favour, because you have the ability to understand the long-term implications of the position and to formulate long range plans.

Before giving concrete advice on how to treat your chess computer in the endgame, let us first show an example of how horribly computer programs can play in the endgame. This game was played in the 1986 ACM (North American) Computer Chess Championship in Dallas, a tournament in which all of the contestants were computer programs.

REX–VAXCHESS
Dallas, 1986

To the uninitiated this position, with White to move, appears to be a straightforward win for White, who is two pawns ahead and has the advantage of the two bishops. As you play through the remainder of this game you will notice that REX fails to take account of the potential strength of Black's h-pawn!

38 ♖c6 ♗e7 39 ♖hc1 ♖d8 40 ♖c8 ♘xh5

So now Black has a passed pawn! It is not easy to be certain exactly why White allowed its h-pawn to be captured, but I suspect that its arithmetic was something like this:

isolated pawn penalty (for its h-pawn) +
bonus for having doubled rooks on the open c-file +
bonus for getting a rook to the 7th rank
> the value of a pawn

41 ♖1c7 ♘f6 42 ♗c4 ♘e8 43 ♖xd8 ♗xd8 44 ♖c8 ♔e7 45 ♗d2 ♖h5 46 a4 ♗b6 47 ♗e3 ♘d6 48 ♖c6 ♗a5

Now White enters into a series of exchanges. After all, everyone knows that you should trade pieces when you are ahead in the endgame!

49 ♖c5 ♖xc5 50 dxc5 ♘xc4 51 bxc4 h5

Here it comes.

52 ♔b2 h4 53 f3 h3 54 ♗g1 ♗d2 55 ♗h2 ♔d7 56 f5

This move was most likely prompted by the horizon effect. White sees that the c5 pawn will fall and tries to push this loss over its horizon.

56 ... exf5 57 ♔b3 ♗e3 58 ♔b4 ♔c6 59 ♔c3 ♗xc5 60 a5 g5 61 ♔b3 g4 62 fxg4 ♗d6 63 ♗g1 fxg4 64 a6 h2 65 ♗xh2 ♗xh2 White Resigns

The moral to this sad story is that the computer's greatest endgame weakness lies in its failure to treat the creation and/or advance of an enemy passed pawn as a serious matter. You can take advantage of this by encouraging the computer to concentrate its forces on one side of the board, where it can pick up a pawn or two, while you create a passed pawn as far as possible from the centre of action. In particular, try to create the passed pawn on the opposite wing from the computer's king — by the time it realises that it needs its king to catch the passed pawn, it may be too late for the computer to regroup its forces.

Having derided the way that computers often fail to understand the strength of passed pawns, we should perhaps redress the balance somewhat by warning you about those aspects of endgame play at which your computer can shine. Firstly, you should remember that in the endgame there are fewer moves, on average, than in the middlegame. This means that with the same average amount of time at its disposal, your computer will be able to search to a greater depth in the endgame.

You should therefore take even greater care when analyzing tactical endgame variations.

Another point to watch out for is that nowadays many programs have an algorithm for bringing their king towards the "most important" pawns. This is sometimes accomplished by giving each of the pawns on the board a weight (or value) — passed pawns are worth the most — and then encouraging the king to wander towards the "centre of mass" of these pawns. This simple programming device is quite effective and often makes the program appear to understand what is happening in the game. In order to fool the program into moving its king to the wrong part of the board, you need to make it think that the pawn which you intend to promote is unimportant and that the pawns on the other wing are much more significant. This can sometimes be achieved by deliberately creating slight weaknesses in your pawn formation on one wing, so as to distract the computer. When it goes after your weaknesses you immediately rush to create a passed pawn elsewhere.

4　What Comes Next?

Unless you chose unwisely when buying your chess computer the chances are that, even with all the good advice in this book, you will take some time before you are able to defeat it regularly on its strongest playing level. As you work your way up, level by level, your own chess ability will improve. In fact we believe that regular practice against your chess computer, playing a variety of openings as White and Black, is one of the very best ways of improving your chess. But what do you do with your chess computer once you have mastered the art of beating it? Should you give it away, sell it or consign it to the back of a cupboard? None of these! You still benefit enormously from the computer if you use it as an analytical assistant. Here are some ideas that will help you to improve the overall standard of your game, using your computer as an aide.

How to Improve Your Chess

Chess computers and chess programs running on personal computers can be extremely useful in improving the standard of play of any human who is not stronger than the program's top playing level. Even for rank beginners, people who do not know how the pieces move, a chess program is in many ways the ideal teacher — it never gets tired, it never gets bored, it never refuses to play another game and it will never allow the user to make an illegal move. (At least this should be the case, but it was not always so. A number of chess computers of the first generation would allow the opponent to make illegal moves and would occasionally do so themselves. For example, I once won a game against a computer in two moves by playing 1 ♘g1–e5!! d7–d6 2 a2xf7 mate, whereupon the computer signalled "You win"!)

Experiments conducted in Holland with a group of women who did not know the rules of the game showed that after two months with a chess computer, and no human help, most of the women had made extremely good progress. Since the cheapest chess computers now cost no more than about £20 and programs for personal computers are available for as little as £6 (although you also need the personal computer) anyone who wishes to learn chess need not pay too much for the privilege.

For those who are already familiar with the game, and wish to become stronger, we would like to suggest some ideas that will almost certainly help. Let us first consider how a chess program can be used to improve your opening play.

The Openings

Choose an opening or a variation that you wish to study. If your chess program is one of the better ones it will have a reasonably sized openings library, so the first thing to do is to play a large number of games against the computer, as both Black and White, with your chosen opening. The openings books in most programs have some sort of randomisation, so if you want to play against the Sicilian Defence your computer will sometimes thwart you by replying to your 1 e2–e4 with a move other than 1 ... c7–c5. If this happens simply start a new game until you get the desired response. *Most programs, however, will allow you to enter the first few moves of an opening and then play from the desired position.*

At first you should play fairly fast games with the chosen opening, to familiarise yourself with some of the variations stored in the program's openings book, and to get accustomed to the type of positions that arise in a particular opening. It is as well to play whole games, rather than stop when the middle or endgame is reached, because in order to gain a deep insight into an opening it is necessary to have a good feel for the various motifs that occur time and time again — i.e. the way that White can attack the black king; the way that Black can establish a strongly posed knight on d4; whatever are the key ideas in the opening, you need to see them repeatedly, from both sides of the board.

When this familiarisation process has been completed, play some more games with this opening but at slower speeds, increasing the playing level of the program steadily and playing a number of games with the opening at each level, taking White and Black in turn. By the time that you have played a number of games at a level which responds in 2–3 minutes per move, you will know just as much as your computer opponent about the chosen opening.

The next stage is to start to think for yourself in the opening, to devise new ideas and new strategies and to find "new" moves (moves which are not in the book). When you find what you think is a good, original idea, make a note of it, then try playing the idea against the program. Play several games with the same idea, at different levels, and try to keep a note of the moves of these games. If the idea appears to be unsuccessful, reverse the colours and adopt whatever strategy the computer used to refute your idea. If the refutation is adequate, the program will not be able to survive against you, but if the program manages to avoid the problems that beset you from the other side of the board, switch colours again and *use the program's ideas to beat it at its own game.*

This method will teach you a lot about the particular opening that you have chosen, and it will help you to explore any new ideas in the opening which you are planning to play in club competitions or tournaments. You will be able to keep a file of games that you have played with this opening against the computer, and you should try to construct your own tree of the opening, on paper, nominating terminal positions when the situation is clear or when the middlegame has been reached, and writing your own assessment of the terminal positions on the tree measured in (say) hundredths of a pawn. If your chess computer can provide you with its own evaluation of a position, so much the better. You can record this evaluation alongside your own assessment.

When you are satisfied that you have done as much work on the variation as you need to, and when your tree has enough information to be useful to you, try to find an openings monograph devoted entirely to the opening or variation in question (we would recommend the Batsford series of openings monographs). Look to see how your own assessments and those of the computer compared with what is on the printed page, and study the book further to increase your understanding of the opening.

The Middlegame

One method of middlegame training, which has worked well for the Soviet school of chess, is for the student to make a detailed study of a chess position, writing down his analysis and producing a systematic report on the position. This method lends itself well to computerisation and readers of this book can employ the same approach to the benefit of their own middlegame abilities.

Select a middlegame position from a master game published in a chess book or magazine. Try to find a game which has been annotated in great depth by a strong player, for example Larsen's own notes to the games in his book *Master of Counter-Attack* (Batsford) or Alekhine's classic annotations to his games in *Alekhine's Greatest Games of Chess* (Batsford). Play through a game up to the point where you are at the bottom of the right hand page, but do not turn the page. This is very important, because you should avoid knowing the next move and you should also avoid seeing any of the analysis that occurs later in the game. You should also ensure that the position does not allow an obvious capture of material (for example, a forced recapture) and that the next move is not forced for any other reason, such as getting out of check. Make a note of the position and study it for about half an hour, moving the pieces around on the board as you do so. You are now ready to begin your detailed analysis of the position, using your chess computer as your partner in analysis.

Make a list of the moves you consider plausible for the player whose turn it is to move next, and sort them into descending order of merit, so that the best move is at the top of your list. Now set up the position on your chess computer, at its lowest level, and ask it to compute the next move. When it has done so, make a note of the move chosen by the computer and the level at which it was thinking, and increase the level before taking back the move and asking the program to think again. Repeat this at each level of play, so that you have the computer's responses for a range of thinking times (6–8 levels is sufficient, ranging from 1 or 2 seconds per move, up to 3 minutes or slightly more).

Make a note of which of your own moves were also chosen by the computer, and which level the computer was set at for each of those moves. Then produce another sorted move list including your own list and the moves selected by the computer. You may decide to reorder some of the moves in your own list, in the light of new information provided by the computer, and you may decide to reject some of the computer's moves (particularly those suggested at very fast levels) if they obviously lose material or allow mate.

Now that you have a sorted move list, based on your own ideas and the ideas of the computer, take the top move in this list and examine the resulting position. Study this position for about thirty minutes and list the moves which you consider plausible. Ask your computer for its opinion at each playing level, and once again produce a sorted list containing your own moves and those suggested by the computer.

When you have done this for each of the plausible moves in the root position (the position taken from the book or magazine), you may decide to reorder the list to some extent. You should then take the top move on the list from the root position, and the top move on the list in reply to that move, and analyse the resulting 2-ply position in the same way. From now on, every time you complete and sort the list of moves from any position, examine the tree which you are producing and determine which is the path that represents the best play for both sides. When you are satisfied that the top move in the list from the root position is the correct move to play, turn over the page of the book and see how your own analysis compares with the analysis by the author and with what actually happened in the game. You should allow several hours for the whole task, preferably conducted in one session. As your own play improves, you will find that you are putting fewer and fewer moves on your plausibility list, and when this number averages 1.7 or thereabouts (and includes the best move almost every time), you will be Grandmaster strength!

The Endgame

It is well known that chess programs play the endgame rather less well than they play in the middlegame. The same is true of most human players, but the disparity is much greater in computer programs. It is therefore rather more difficult to use your chess program to help you improve your endgame, than is the case for the opening or the middlegame. Nevertheless, there do exist one or two possibilities for self improvement using one of the stronger chess programs.

Probably the most basic help that can be gleaned from a computer is the technique for forcing mate with very little material on the board. Beginners find it difficult to mate with king and queen against king, and with king and rook against king. More experienced players can conclude the game rather easily given one of these combinations of pieces, but some still find difficulty in mating with king and two bishops against king, or with king, bishop and knight against king. Here a computer program can help, but only one of the strongest ones.

Some chess computers can force mate with the two bishops and with bishop and knight. The human player who wishes to polish up his technique in these standard mating configurations can do a lot worse than practice against a computer. First try to mate the computer, and it will try to make life as difficult for you as possible. If you do not succeed within the confines of the 50 move rule, or if you do succeed but find it difficult to do so, then try playing with the king and see how the computer drives your king to the corner (the correct corner in the case of bishop and knight), and then mates you. When you have experienced this treatment two or three times, try again to mate the computer. Continue repeating this cycle until you find that you can always force mate.

At a less basic level you can try to analyse endgame positions using the same process as was described for the middlegame. You will not benefit quite so much as you will when studying the middlegame, because the computer will tend to be less useful in adding genuinely plausible moves to your list, but the exercise should still prove worthwhile.

5 The Computer Triumphs?

Grandmasters are coming under increasing siege from chess computers. Hans Berliner, the guru of computer chess in the USA, is on record as predicting that within four years computers will be able to outplay the human World Champion. The win by DEEP THOUGHT against Bent Larsen in America 1988 fuels such fears, and Gary Kasparov now believes that his mission in life is to defend mankind against the best chess programs.

Nevertheless, succour is perhaps at hand. Professor Donald Michie, the UK's very own Computer Magus, pointed out that although the top computers now well may possess "over 700,000 nodes of look-ahead tree per second" that they may well be vulnerable to: "computer hostile modes of play, historically pioneered by International Master David Levy." In a forthcoming academic paper Professor Michie states: "When pitted against a chess program Levy adopts a style which he described as — do nothing — but do it very well. Although not effective against human masters, it scores heavily against computer opponents. By going for blocked positions devoid of tactical mobility he invites his computer opponent to reveal its threadbare positional sense and lack of long range strategic ideas. Sooner or later, the machine drifts into some position which it is incapable of recognising as strategically doomed. Before this happens, however, a stronger, but less computer-wise player than Levy would yield to the temptation to try some tactics – and become lost in calculational complexities."

The following game shows how dangerous it is to face machines on their own territory, open tactical battles. White is a commercial micro on sale in the shops, not a big academic mainframe. Black is one of the members of the twice Olympic Gold Medal winning

Hungarian Women's team, yet she is roundly slaughtered by the metal monster.

NOVAG SUPER EXPERT–
Ildiko Madl
Aubervilliers (Rapid), 1988

1	e4	c5
2	♘f3	d6
3	d4	cxd4
4	♘xd4	♘f6
5	♘c3	♘c6
6	♗g5	e6
7	♕d2	a6
8	0–0–0	♗d7
9	f4	h6
10	♗h4	g5

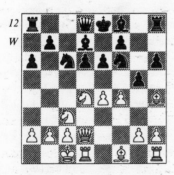

12
W

Even Black's opening is a misguided choice against a computer. The Sicilian is a double-edged weapon, and what Black has ventured represents a singularly double-edged subset of it. Madl would have been better advised to select the strategic Caro–Kann. As we shall see, though, this advice does not necessarily apply to Kasparov!

11	fxg5	♘g4
12	♘f3	hxg5

Now after 13 ♗xg5 f6 14 ♗f4 e5 Black wins due to the threat of ... ♗h6.

13	♗g3	♗e7
14	♗e2	♘ge5
15	♔b1	♘xf3
16	♗xf3	♘e5
17	♗xe5	dxe5
18	♕e2	♕b6
19	♗h5	♗a3?

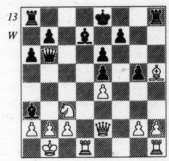

13
W

This sort of move, threatening mate, might unnerve a human opponent, but computers have no nerves, and the "Super Expert" now finds a neat tactical sequence which not only nets a pawn but also exposes the black king. Ultimately, Black's pawn on f7 is indefensible, so the best course would have been to sacrifice it at once with 19 ... 0–0–0 20 ♗xf7 ♗c5 planning ... ♗d4. If then 21 ♕c4 ♔b8 22 ♖xd7 ♖xd7 23 ♘a4 ♕d6!

and the threat of ... ♛d1+ wins for Black.

20   ♗xf7+!   ♚e7

If 20 ... ♚xf7, then 21 ♖xd7+ ♚e8 22 ♘a4 ♛c6 23 ♖d3 wins a pawn.

21	b3	♖ad8
22	♖df1	♛d4
23	♛f3	♛c5
24	♛f6+	♚d6
25	♘d5	♖df8
26	♖d1	♚c6
27	♛g6	♖xf7

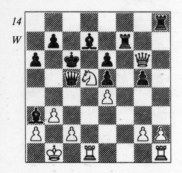

14
W

In a bad position Black makes a faulty combination.

28	♛xf7	exd5
29	♛f6+	♚c7
30	♛xe5+	♚b6
31	♛xh8	♗b4
32	♖xd5	♛c6
33	♛d8+	1–0

Here we see how even a world-famous Grandmaster such as Bent Larsen can be defeated by a top computer due to the adoption of poor tactics.

Larsen–DEEP THOUGHT
Long Beach, California, 1988

1 c4 e5 2 g3 ♘f6 3 ♗g2 c6 4 ♘f3 e4 5 ♘d4 d5 6 cxd5 ♛xd5 7 ♘c2 ♛h5 8 h4 ♗f5 9 ♘e3 ♗c5 10 ♛b3 b6 11 ♛a4 0–0 12 ♘c3 b5 13 ♛c2 ♗xe3 14 dxe3 ♖e8 15 a4 b4 16 ♘b1 ♘bd7 17 ♘d2 ♖e6 18 b3 ♖d8 19 ♗b2 ♗g6 20 ♘c4 ♘d5 21 0–0–0 ♘7f6 22 ♗h3 ♗f5 23 ♗xf5 ♛xf5 24 f3 h5 25 ♗d4 ♖d7 26 ♚b2 ♖c7 27 g4 hxg4 28 ♖hg1 c5 29 fxg4 ♘xg4 30 ♗xg7 ♖g6 31 ♛d2 ♖d7 32 ♖xg4 ♖xg4 33 ♘e5 ♘xe3 34 ♛xd7 ♘xd1+ 35 ♛xd1 ♖g3 36 ♛d6 ♚xg7 37 ♘d7 ♖e3 38 ♛h2 ♚h7 39 ♘f8+ ♚h8 40 h5 ♛d5 41 ♘g6+ fxg6 42 hxg6+ ♚g7 43 ♛h7+ ♚f6 **White resigns.**

Professor Michie, apropos the following Dominic Lawson game against DEEP THOUGHT: "About a month after DEEP THOUGHT defeated Larsen, an informal exploration of DEEP THOUGHT's other parts revealed a surprising lack of resource in dealing with a player grounded in the Levy style. Dominic Lawson is a former British County player, informally assessed as being in the 2250 range. He was given an hour or so's briefing by Levy prior to engaging DEEP THOUGHT in a 30 minute game. Eventually Lawson got into severe time trouble and lost, but not before his do-nothing policy had elicited from DEEP THOUGHT sufficiently poor play to place the program in extreme jeopardy."

Interestingly, in this game White, forewarned by the debacle suffered by Bent Larsen, and tutored in advance by David Levy, adopted a sensibly restrained strategic approach. By doing this, White brought the machine to the very edge of defeat. Things only began to go wrong when both sides' allotted time started to run out. At this point the human player committed a series of tactical errors, caused by the necessity of calculating variations with only a few minutes available.

Dominic Lawson–DEEP THOUGHT
played by Transatlantic telephone link, December 1988

(Half an hour to each player for all the moves)

1	♘f3	d5
2	d4	♘f6
3	♗f4	

A sensible opening to adopt against a computer. First it disengages the machine from its 'book'; additionally, it creates a strategic type of position rather than an open tactical one in which computers might excel.

3	...	♘c6?

Already DEEP THOUGHT commits a strategic error. It is suspect to block the c-pawn thus in queenside openings. 3 ... c5 is both obvious and playable. A parallel example, with the defence handled by a great master of the Classical school, was the game Janowsky–Tarrasch, Ostend 1905. This had gone 1 d4 d5 2 ♘f3 c5 3 c3 e6 4 ♗f4 ♕b6 5 ♕b3 ♘f6 6 e3 ♘c6 7 h3 ♗e7 8 ♘bd2 ♗d7 9 ♗e2 0–0 10 0–0 ♖fc8 with equality.

4	e3	♘h5
5	♗g3	

There is nothing wrong with 5 ♗g5 h6 6 ♗h4 g5 7 ♗g3.

5	...	♘xg3
6	hxg3	e6
7	♗b5	♗d7
8	c3	

Perhaps more accurate is 8 ♘bd2 developing a piece, keeping the option of c4 and giving the additional option of ♕e2 in White's arsenal.

8	...	♗d6
9	♘bd2	f5

To prevent White from playing e4.

10	♘h4	

Threatens ♕h5+ and so forces Black's hand, for if Black plays the

natural 10 ... ♛f6 11 ♛f5+ g6 12 ♘xg6! ♛xg6 13 ♛xg6+ hxg6 14 ♖xh8+ wins outright.

10   ...   0-0
11   ♗a4

This keeps the Bishop defended, but 11 f4 planning ♗d3 and g4 to attack on the kingside, looks more natural.

11   ...   ♛e8

The computer plays another ungainly move mainly because it can become part of a concrete tactical variation. There is no other discernable merit in 11 ...

♛e8. DEEP THOUGHT is speculating on tactical traps aimed at White's bishop on a4.

12   0-0

Setting a trap based on the predilection for forcing variations evinced by DEEP THOUGHT.

12   ...   g5

This does not win material and is therefore strategically suspect. However from DEEP THOUGHT's point of view it forces events.

13   ♘hf3   ♘xd4

Not necessary by any means, but it is the logical follow up to the previous move.

14   ♗xd7   ♘xf3+
15   ♘xf3   ♛xd7
16   ♘xg5   ♖f6

The point of this is not clear. Black has no real prospect of launching an attack in the h-file.

17   ♖c1!

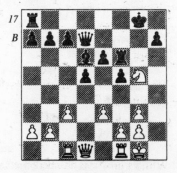

Preparing to punch holes in Black's centre. This is the type of quiet strategic play which DEEP THOUGHT cannot readily handle.

17	...	♖g6
18	♘f3	b5?

An exceedingly dubious advance which actually undermines Black's own centre. DEEP THOUGHT is trying to stop White from playing c4, but this goal is impracticable. Correct would have been 18 ... c6 to strengthen the Black centre.

19	b3

Consistently steering for the key advance c4.

19	...	c5?

Totally inappropriate. Black must keep the defensive resource ... c6 in reserve. This megalomaniac seizure of territory is completely wrong, not least since it places a target pawn on the c5-square which impedes the scope of Black's bishop.

20	c4!

The logical follow up to White's 17th and 19th moves.

20	...	bxc4

Not 20 ... dxc4 when 21 ♘e5 wins material.

21	bxc4	♕f7
22	♖b1	

White's position has become so good that he suffers from an embarrassment of choices over the next few moves. The text is excel-

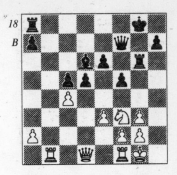

lent, in that it occupies an important open file. Nonetheless, 22 ♕d2 or 22 cxd5 exd5 23 ♕d3 were also highly tempting. The latter embodies the powerful threats of ♘h4 or ♖fd1, pressing against Black's sensitive pawns on d5 and f5.

22	...	♖d8
23	♕a4	dxc4
24	♕xc4	♖g4
25	♕a6	♖b4

This reduces some of the pressure. After the trade on b4 Black acquires a queenside pawn majority. Nevertheless, Black's position remains full of holes and suffers from the disadvantage of numerous scattered pawn islands.

26	♖xb4	cxb4
27	♖d1	♕e7
28	♕c4	h6
29	♖d4!	♖d7
30	♕d3	♖d8
31	♘e5!	

A powerful invasion which overloads Black's resources and

leaves DEEP THOUGHT without sufficient defence. Ominously, though, White was becoming very short of time. Black cannot now of course, play 31 ... ♗xe5 on account of 32 ♖xd8+

31   ...   ♛c7

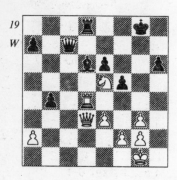

19
W

32   ♘c4?

32 ♛b3! ♗xe5 33 ♛xe6+ ♔f8 (best) 34 ♛xf5+ ♔e7 35 ♖e4 wins for White. It should be noted that White cannot vary the move order in this decisive sequence. If, erroneously 33 ♖xd8+ ♛xd8 34 ♛xe6+ ♔f8 35 ♛xe5 ♛d1+ 36 ♔h2 ♛h5+ with a draw, while 35 ♛xf5+ fails to ... ♛f6. The move in the text dissipates White's edge. Alternative variations are 32 ♛b3! ♛c8 33 ♘c6 ♛xc6 34 ♛xe6+ ♔g7 35 ♖h4 ♖h8 36 ♛xf5 with a decisive attack, or 32 ♛b3! ♖e8 33 ♘d3 a5 34 g4 fxg4 35 ♖xg4+ when the black position is a mess.

32   ...   ♗e7
33   ♔f1?

This accomplishes nothing but the exposure of White's king. 33 g4 is good.

33   ...   ♖xd4
34   ♛xd4   h5
35   ♔e2?

Asking for trouble.

35   ...   ♗f6!

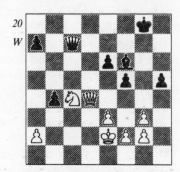

20
W

Just right. This blow demolishes what remains of White's central domination. If now 36 ♛xf6 ♛xc4+ 37 ♔e1 ♛c1+ 38 ♔e2 ♛c2+ 39 ♔e1 ♛b1+ and ♛xa2 with check. The only chance therefore, is 39 ♔f3 and if 39 ... ♛xa2 40 ♛d8+ draws, while 39 ... ♛d1+ 40 ♔f4 offers nothing clear to Black.

36   ♛d3?

After this White is rapidly tied in knots and it is impressive to see how well DEEP THOUGHT handles positions where: a) it has the advantage; b) the situation is open; and c) simplification has made pure calculation easier.

36   ...   ♛c6

37	♔f1	♕a6
38	♕c2	♗c3

Locking White in.

39	♕b3	♕b5
40	♔g1	♕d5

The retreat by White's king into the shelter of its kingside pawns underscores just how futile was its centralisation at moves 33 and 35.

41 ♘a5?

Premature desperation. There were still real drawing chances to be had with 41 ♔h2, tucking the king away, e.g. 41 ... a5 42 ♘xa5 ♕xa5 43 ♕xe6+ netting a valuable extra pawn in comparison with the game continuation. Alternatively, 41 ♔h2 ♔f7 42 a3 a5 43 axb4 axb4 44 ♕a2 when Black's king is hard to shield from checks.

41	...	♕xa5
42	♕xe6+	♔g7
43	♕e7+	♔g6
44	♕e8+	♔f6

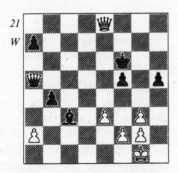

21
W

And in this probably lost position, White overstepped the time limit, thus losing the game.

Here are a couple of games in which the former World Championship finalist, David Bronstein, game to grief in a mixed human/computer tournament.

Bronstein–HITECH
Amsterdam, 1990

1 d4 d5 2 c4 dxc4 3 e4 e5 4 ♘f3 exd4 5 ♗xc4 ♘c6 6 0-0 ♗e6 7 ♗xe6 fxe6 8 ♕b3 ♕d7 9 ♕xb7 ♖b8 10 ♕a6 ♘f6 11 ♘bd2 ♗b4 12 ♕d3 ♗xd2 13 ♘xd2 0-0 14 a3 ♘e5 15 ♕g3 ♘h5 16 ♕h4 ♘f4 17 b4 ♘e2+ 18 ♔h1 ♘d3 19 ♘b3 ♕a4 20 ♘c5 ♘xf2+ 21 ♕xf2 ♖xf2 22 ♖e1 ♕c2 23 ♗g5 ♘g3+ 24 hxg3 ♖xg2 0-1

Bronstein–MEPHISTO 68030
Amsterdam, 1990

1 b3 d5 2 ♗b2 c5 3 e3 ♘f6 4 ♘f3 ♗g4 5 h3 ♗h5 6 g4 ♗g6 7 ♘e5 ♘bd7 8 ♘xg6 hxg6 9 ♗g2 e6 10 g5 ♘h5 11 c4 ♕xg5 12 ♕g4 ♕d8 13 cxd5 ♘hf6 14 ♗xf6 ♕xf6 15 dxe6 ♕xa1 16 exd7+ ♔d8 17 ♕e4 ♗d6 18 ♔e2 ♕xa2 19 ♕xb7 ♖b8 20 ♕c6 ♗c7 21 ♖c1 ♕xb3 22 ♘c3 ♕c4+ 23 ♔d1 ♖b6 24 ♕a8+ ♗b8 25 ♘d5 ♕a4+ 26 ♔e2 ♖b2 27 ♖xc5 ♕xd7 28 f4 ♖h5 29 ♖c3 ♖xh3 30 ♔f2 ♕g4 0-1

Before we look at some games in which mankind fared rather better, let's see how computers battle against each other.

6 Machine Against Machine

In Alan Ayckbourn's futuristic play, 'HENCEFORWARD', a character at one point asks why humans are actually superior to machines. In chess terms, at least, the conventional answer is that human players are blessed with imagination, while computers can only calculate. But what if imagination and intuition really amount to inspired guesswork, and what if inspired guesswork is ultimately proven to be inadequate when confronted by flawless calculation.

I had never truly believed that computers would defeat Grandmasters, but that breakthrough has now occurred. DEEP THOUGHT, programmed largely by Feng-hsiung Hsu of Carnegie-Mellon University in the States, won a strong tournament in 1988, tying with our excompatriot Grandmaster Tony Miles, and defeating the great Bent Larsen en route.

Even more remarkable, perhaps, is the thought that commercial micro-computers are virtually keeping pace with the big academic number-crunchers. In the North American Computer Chess Championship, which shortly preceded the Thanksgiving event, DEEP THOUGHT could only share first prize with a commercial Fidelity model. Here is one game where machine met machine from that tournament. For most of the game it was DEEP THOUGHT which was under pressure from the commercial machine.

MEPHISTO–DEEP THOUGHT
North American Computer Chess Championship, Orlando, 1988

| 1 | c4 | e5 |
| 2 | ♘c3 | ♗b4 |

A risky move, which gives White the opportunity to chase the black bishop with gain of time, or to acquire the bishop pair in a relatively open position.

3 ♘d5 ♗a5

The best retreat square. If instead Black opts for the artificial 3 ... ♗d6 then 4 d4 gives White the advantage.

4	b4	c6
5	bxa5	cxd5
6	cxd5	♕xa5

Theory suggests that Black might interpose 6 ... ♘f6 but after 7 ♕b3 ♕xa5 8 ♘f3 d6 9 ♗a3! White still has the edge, as in the game Smejkal–Dely, Carlovy Hradec 1981. Perhaps there is some mileage in not retrieving the pawn, e.g., 6 ... ♘f6 7 ♕b3 0–0!? DEEP THOUGHT decides to take back the pawn at once. MEPHISTO could now have transposed into the Smejkal game with 7 ♕b3, but the move chosen is also interesting.

7 e4 d6

7 ... ♘f6 is more accurate, before White develops his queen's bishop.

8	♗b2	♘f6
9	♗c3	♕d8
10	♗b5+	♘bd7
11	d3	a6
12	♗xd7+	♗xd7
13	♘e2	♖c8
14	0–0	0–0
15	♕d2	b5

Strategically White should play 16 f4 but 16 ... ♕b6+ 17 ♔h1 ♘g4 makes life messy. It is, therefore, correct to prevent the black

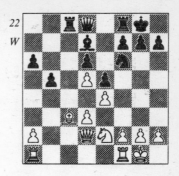

22 W

queen from reaching the a7–g1 diagonal.

16 ♗a5 ♕e7

Now is the time for White to play 17 f4 with a clear strategic edge. Instead, White seeks to trade all the rooks.

17 f3 ♘h5

Very interesting here is 17 g4 for if 18 ... ♘f4 19 ♘xf4 ♕g5 20 ♗b4. And if 18 ... ♘f6 19 ♘g3 and White has a big edge. However MEPHISTO sticks to its plan.

18	♖ac1	f5
19	♖xc8	♖xc8
20	♖c1	♘f6
21	♗b4	♕d8
22	♖xc8	♗xc8
23	♗a5	♕e7
24	♕c1	♗b7
25	♘g3	g6
26	♗b6	♔f7
27	♘e2	♔g7
28	♗a5	h5
29	♔h1	♔f7
30	h3	♔g7

31	♕e3	♔h7
32	♕b6	♘e8
33	♘c3	♕d7
34	♔g1	♔g7

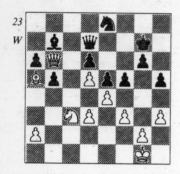

23
W

MEPHISTO is obviously better, the black king is rather exposed and all White's pieces stand more actively than their black opposite numbers. Still, it is not an easy task to break through.

35	d4	exd4
36	♕xd4+	♔f7
37	♕b6	fxe4
38	fxe4	♕e7
39	♗b4	♔f6
40	♗a3	h4
41	♗c5	♔g5
42	♗e3+	♔h5
43	♕d4	g5

White's next move is absolutely incredible although it is not a losing blunder. It is, however, a very stupid move to which no human master would warrant more than a passing glance. 44

24
W

a4 simply grants Black a passed pawn, for no compensating advantage position. I [RDK] am no expert in the "psychology" of machine players, but my guess is as follows: MEPHISTO had had a good position for a long time. But it does not know how to try for a win, hence the endless toing and froing, the subtle varying of the position, but without any tangible success.

Now, MEPHISTO has simply run out of ideas completely, and therefore plays a move which radically changes the structure of the position without, however, forfeiting its general type of advantage, and without ceding DEEP THOUGHT serious winning prospects. Much stronger in any case is 44 ♕h8+ and if 44 ... ♔g6 45 ♕g8+ ♘g7 46 ♗d4.

44	a4	bxa4
45	♕xa4	♘f6
46	♗d4	♔g6
47	♕c2	♗c8

To meet 48 e5+ with ♗f5.

48	♕d3	♔f7
49	♕f1	♗d7
50	♕f3	a5
51	♕e3	♔g6
52	♕d3	♔f7
53	♕f3	a4
54	♕e3	♔g6
55	♕d3	♔h6
56	♕b1	a3
57	♔h2	a2
58	♕xa2	♘xe4
59	♕c2	♗f5

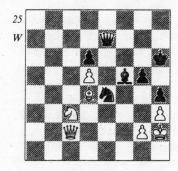

The position must now be drawn. White has pussyfooted around long enough and has to force the issue. 60 ♘xe4 is necessary, after which the game would be a draw. If 60 ... ♕xe4 61 ♕xe4 ♗xe4 62 ♗f6 and White rounds up the black d-pawn. Alternatively, 60 ... ♗xe4 61 ♕e2 pinning the bishop — and there are other moves to draw — is quite OK. I cannot understand why here White persistently avoids a draw and decentralises its pieces. Is it

perhaps possible that MEPHISTO had to win this game and therefore had been programmed to sidestep draws at all costs? I simply do not know the answer to this question. Suffice it to say, 60 ♘b5 is a very bad move, and DEEP THOUGHT now starts a winning attack against White's denuded king.

60	♘b5	♕f7
61	♕c4	♗d7
62	♔g1	♕f4
63	♘a3	♘d2
64	♕d3	♗f5
65	♕c3	♗xh3

DEEP THOUGHT is in its element, brutal calculation in an open position. This move wins a pawn and strips away the protection from around the white king.

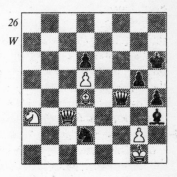

| 66 | ♗g7+ | ♔h5 |

If now 67 gxh3 ♕f1+ 68 ♔h2 g4 and ... g3 wins.

| 67 | ♕d3 | ♗xg2 |

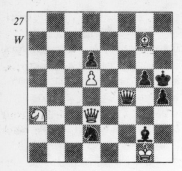

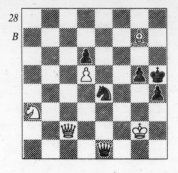

In diagram 27, we see the final winning sacrifice. I am sure that any strong human would play this "knowing" that it led to a forced win, without necessarily calculating all the variations in advance. I equally suspect that DEEP THOUGHT worked out all the ramifications in advance to checkmate before making this sacrifice.

68	♔xg2	♕g4+
69	♔h1	♘e4
70	♕c2	♕h3+
71	♔g1	♕e3+
72	♔h1	♕e1+
73	♔g2	*(28)*

and White resigned,

somewhat unconventionally announcing mate in seven moves against itself. 73 ... h3+ and 73 ... g4 are both adequate to achieve this. White has to make heavy material sacrifices even to last this long.

MEPHISTO lost the game, from a somewhat superior position, through an almost human obstinacy in refusing to play for a draw. Both 44 a4 and 60 ♘b5 were excessively ambitious. After the latter move White is probably lost. DEEP THOUGHT is, though, clearly the stronger machine. The opening was unfortunate and left Black almost totally devoid of active possibilities. Once the situation opened up, however, DEEP THOUGHT rapidly demonstrated its superiority. We hear that Hans Berliner has predicted that in 3–4 years a computer will be stronger than the human World Champion.

In 1989, DEEP THOUGHT won the World Computer Championship for the first time. The key game was against Hans Berliner's HITECH in the last round. HITECH cunningly used the same opening with which Dominic Lawson, Deputy Editor of *The Spectator* magazine, constructed a winning position against DEEP THOUGHT in their telephone game some months previously. In this game, DEEP THOUGHT committed the same error of blocking its c-pawn with a knight in the opening. Nevertheless, major league dithering by HI-TECH in the middle game threw away the full point and later even the draw. DEEP THOUGHT's conduct of the concluding attack was forceful.

HITECH–DEEP THOUGHT
6th World Computer-Chess Championship, Edmonton, 1989

1	d4	d5
2	♘f3	♞f6

White's next move makes me think that HITECH's programmers must have been well aware of the opening of the Lawson game. DEEP THOUGHT got such a terrible position against this apparently harmless old line of the Queen's pawn opening that the temptation to repeat it must have been enormous.

3 ♗f4!

The exclamation point is, of course, relative. This move of the queen's bishop would be less effective against a booked-up human player. The problem for DEEP THOUGHT, of course, is that the opening variation is so offbeat that it probably does not

figure in its memory banks at all. DEEP THOUGHT is, therefore, strategically on its own in the early stages, and it does some terrible things.

3 ... e6

There is actually little wrong with the blocking in of the black queen's bishop like this, but 3 ... ♗f5 is also playable. The real error comes at the next move.

4 e3 ♞c6?

There is a perfectly valid rule which states that one must not block the c-pawn with a knight in queenside openings, since this impedes the liberating move ... c5. Naturally, there are exceptions, such as Tchigorin's defence, 1 d4 d5 2 c4 ♞c6, which is just about regarded as respectable. Nevertheless, the rule is a good one and I do not understand why DEEP THOUGHT has not been programmed with the basic precept, the more so since it committed the same error in the Lawson game.

5	♘bd2	♗e7
6	h3	0–0
7	♗e2	♞h5?

Once again an idea from the game against Lawson crops up, but here in a crasser form. In the earlier game there was a real chance that this knight manoeuvre would catch the white queen's bishop. Here the white bishop can just retire safely to h2 (the point of HITECH's 6th move) from where it can train its sights on the black queen's wing, especially on the target pawn on c7.

8 &h2!

It may seem strange to award this obvious retreat an exclamation mark, but in view of the monstrosity perpetrated by HITECH on move 10, I think it deserves credit here for sliding its bishop out of danger. Evidently, the white queen's bishop is worth more than the black king's knight.

8 ... g6

Tactically perceptive but strategically awful, since this move undermines all of the black king's dark squares. In fact, better would have been simple withdrawal by ... &f6. The tactical point which DEEP THOUGHT spotted does, however, deserve some elucidation. Let us suppose that Black had proceeded instead with 8 ... f5 (which comes one move later in the game). Then 9 &e5 &xe5 10 dxe5 leaves Black's knight stranded, while 9 &e5 &f6 10 &xc6 allows White to double the black c-pawns. This must have been the process which prompted DEEP THOUGHT to defend its knight on h5 in advance.

9 0–0 f5

Black's 9th move is another strategically dubious decision

which more or less completely wrecks its own dark square complex on the king's wing. Perhaps Black was trying to play ... f4 or was trying to stop White playing e4. In any case, the correct response would have been 10 c4! with the follow-up &c1, putting pressure on the c-file against the black knight and ultimately the c-pawn, which stands as a weakness behind it. After 10 c4! f4, White can calmly play 11 e4 when both ... dxc4 and ... dxe4 leave White dominant in the centre.

True, White's queen's bishop on h2 would be shut out of play for a while, but the situation of Black's knight on h5 (and this is the piece which would have to support the pawn on f4) is so unstable (White only has to move his f3-knight to open up an attack battery on h5) that the f4-pawn is more of a liability than a source of strength. Instead, White's next move is truly incredible. Clearly bothered by the threat of ... f4 it moves the bishop away from potential, if temporary, incarceration on h2. The effect, though, is threefold strategic disaster.

1. White voluntarily surrenders the bishop pair;
2. White abandons his long-term threats against c7;
3. White frees Black's entire queen's wing by enabling him to trade off the clumsy knight which blocks the black c-pawn. Black inevitably then frees himself with ... c5 in due course.

10	♗e5??	♘xe5
11	♘xe5	♘f6
12	c4	c5?

Having escaped the worst of the opening, Black should consolidate with 12 ... c6. Instead DEEP THOUGHT seizes the centre with pawns, much as in the Lawson game, but here this is quite inappropriate. The freeing thrust ... c5 should be delayed, until Black has achieved a measure of consolidation.

13   ♘df3?

From now on HITECH starts to dither and the degree of hesitation in its play is so extreme that it virtually ceases to have any further genuine influence on the course of the game. It is almost as if there is only one player making moves! White does, in fact, have a very promising course available here, exploiting Black's lack of solid foundation in the centre, the possible weakness of Black's centre pawns, and the vulnerability of the a2–g8 diagonal. Correct is 13 dxc5 ♗xc5 14 cxd5. If now 14 ... exd5 15 ♘b3 ♗d6 16 ♘f3 with very pleasant play against Black's isolated pawn; alternatively, 14 ... ♛xd5 15 ♘dc4 when Black's queenside forces are difficult to develop, while 14 ... ♘xd5 15 ♘df3 followed by developing moves such as ♛b3, ♖ac1, ♖fd1 or ♗c4, makes Black's life exceedingly difficult, due to the looseness of his kingside pawns and his problems mobilizing his queenside pieces. This, in fact, would be a typical Queen's Gambit position where Black had played a lot of extra, but unnecessary and harmful moves, such as ... f5 and ... g6. What White plays is pointless, and Black soon recovers.

13   ...   ♗d6

Now there is still time for White to trade pawns in the centre with advantage, but HITECH can never bring itself to do this.

14   a3   ♛c7

A strong move which surgically removes White's option of dxc5 since the e5 knight would hang.

15	♖c1	a5
16	♛b3	b6
17	♛a4	♗b7

30
W

White's last two feeble moves with the queen are symptomatic of its entire conduct in the game. Henceforth, White's manoeuvres are painful to watch. HITECH clearly has a lot to learn about how to build up strategic positions. The position in diagram 30 represents the best position Black has achieved in the game so far. The Black forces are now well developed, and Black has the long-range plus of the bishop pair, should the centre ever open up.

18	♖c2	♔h8
19	cxd5	♗xd5
20	♖d1	♖ad8
21	♗b5	♘e4

White's next move is a strange adventure. Presumably, the thinking is to plant one knight on d7 and the reserve knight on e5 with a gain of territory. Instead it was necessary to consider 22 ♗c6 to eliminate one of Black's dangerous bishops. In that case Black still has no advantage.

| 22 | ♘d7 | ♖g8 |
| 23 | ♘fe5 | ♖g7 |

Now White's advanced knight is stranded. He is reduced to shuffling around with his rooks.

| 24 | ♖d3 | ♗e7 |
| 25 | ♖d1 | h5 |

Although DEEP THOUGHT wastes some time too, it has now hit on the correct plan. With White's pieces tied down to the salvation of the d7-knight, Black will win by moving forwards his mobile kingside pawns. White now has no choice. It must do something, namely trade pawns on c5. Sadly, HITECH continues to dither with the rooks. Frankly, I cannot understand why the White program plays so incredibly passively in this game.

26	♖dc1?	♗g5
27	♖e1	♗h4
28	♖f1	♗e7
29	♖fc1	g5
30	f3	♘f6

If now 31 ♘xf6 ♗xf6 32 ♘d3 to attack c5, then ... g4 and ... ♕g3 will launch a decisive attack.

| 31 | ♔f1 | g4 |
| 32 | hxg4 | hxg4 *(31)* |

After White's next move, a positional and tactical capitulation, the game is over.

33	f4	♗e4
34	♖d2	♘d5
35	♖e2	♖h7
36	♖ee1	♘xe3+

31
W

37		♔g1

If 37 ♖xe3 ♖h1+

37	...	♘d5
38	♘g6+	♔g7
39	♘xe7	♛xf4

A decisive *intermezzo*. If 40
♘xd5 ♛h2+ mates swiftly.

40	♘xf5+	exf5
41	♖xe4	♛xc1+
42	♗f1	fxe4
43	♛b3	♖h1+
44	♔xh1	♛xf1+
45	♔h2	♖h8+
46	♛h3	g3+
47	♔xg3	♛f4 mate

The conclusion to be drawn is
that DEEP THOUGHT is much
stronger than HITECH. Nevertheless, there is still a very long
way to go in terms of programming its strategic build up in openings which it does not already
know "by heart" as it were.

7 Mankind Strikes Back!

Britain's first ever World Championship semi-finalist, Jon Speelman, turned his talents towards raising funds for the Fight For Sight Charity in early February 1989, when he gave a simultaneous display against no less than 32 opponents. The Grandmaster's final score was an outstanding two losses, six draws and twenty-four wins against powerful opponents, amongst which numbered former European junior champion Shaun Taulbut, and the reigning British Ladies' Champion, Cathy Forbes. Speelman took a mere two hours over this mental exploit. Perhaps the most intriguing game, and certainly the most valuable for chess opening theory, was his clash with the sole computer in the field.

Jon Speelman–NOVAG SUPER EXPERT
Simultaneous Display, London, 1989

1	c4	e5
2	♘c3	♘c6
3	♘f3	♘f6
4	g3	♗b4
5	♗g2	0–0
6	0–0	e4
7	♘g5	♗xc3
8	bxc3	♖e8
9	f3	exf3
10	♘xf3	d5
11	d4	

32
B

The computer is remarkably well versed in this opening, which up to here duplicates the game Kasparov–Ivanchuk from the 1988 Soviet Championship in Moscow. In that earlier game Black had played 11...♘e4, which was met by the World Champion's 12 ♕c2 dxc4 13 ♖b1 f5 14 g4 when White had the makings of a fierce attack. Indeed, Kasparov went on to win the game in just a few more moves. The NOVAG SUPER EXPERT now varies from that precedent with an immediate capture of the gambit pawn.

11 ... dxc4

Speelman's next move is something of a surprise, since the obvious attacking move would be 12 ♗g5, with the intention of capturing on f6 and proceeding with ♘e5.

12 ♖b1 ♕e7

Black increases its pressure along the e-file against White's backward pawn. Indeed, after White's reply, Black should have captured immediately on e2 with 13 ... ♕xe2. As played in the game, White gains some respite from the consequences of what appears to be an inaccurate 12th move.

13	♗f4	♘d5
14	♕c2	♘xf4
15	gxf4	♕e3+
16	♖f2	♘e7

Black avoided the obvious trap of 15 ... ♕xe2, which would fail miserably to 16 ♖be1 ♕xc2 17 ♖xe8 checkmate. As played, Black's threat of ... ♗f5 suddenly seems to be lethal, but Speelman has a cunning way out.

| 17 | ♘e5 | ♗f5 |

18	♕c1!	♕xc1+
19	♖xc1	f6
20	♘xc4	♗e6
21	♘a5	♗xa2
22	♗xb7	♖ab8

33
W

Having recovered from his setback in the opening Speelman now enjoys a clear strategic advantage. This is based on Black's split pawns on the queen's wing and the potential White has for a massive advance of his central pawn majority.

23	e4	♗c4
24	♖a1	♔f7
25	f5	♗d3
26	♖d2	♗b5
27	♔f2	♔f8
28	♔f3	♔f7
29	h4	♘c8
30	c4	♗d7
31	♗d5+	♔e7
32	c5	♖d8
33	♖aa2	♗e8
34	♖ab2	♖b5
35	♖xb5	

34
B

In this position time ran out and the game was adjudicated a win for the White by a panel of experts. Analysis by the computer confirmed this verdict. According to the machine the best line for both sides from the concluding position is 35 ... ♗xb5 36 ♗c6 ♗f1 37 ♔e3 g6 38 ♖b2 gxf5 39 ♖b7 ♔f8 40 ♖xc7 ♘e7 41 d5 ♘xc6 42 ♘xc6 followed by d6, when the white central pawns triumph. This was a fascinating tussle. Mind, or at least the mind of a player of Speelman's class, still triumphs against machine, but for how much longer?

In the rest of this chapter we look at some other examples of successful strategy by mankind against his automated rival.

Ray Keene–NOVAG SUPER EXPERT
Test Blitz Game, London, 1989

1	d4	♘f6
2	♗f4	

We have seen that computers, even DEEP THOUGHT, often react badly to this normally harmless variation. DEEP THOUGHT frequently blocks its c7-pawns by ... ♘c6 (a well known strategic error) while, in general, machines tend to weaken their dark squares against this and similar lines.

2	...	d5
3	e3	

I (Ray) tried 3 c3 in two other games:

(a) 3 c3 e6 4 e3 ♗d6 5 ♗g3 ♗xg3 6 hxg3 ♘bd7 7 ♘bd2 c5 8 ♗d3 ♕b6 9 ♖b1 ♕a5 10 a3 b6 11 ♕e2 ♗b7 12 ♘h3 cxd4 13 exd4 0–0? 14 g4! ♖ac8 15 g5 ♘e8 16 ♗xh7+. A standard sacrifice, with mate, perhaps, beyond the machine's horizon. 16 ... ♔xh7 17 ♕h5+ ♔g8 18 ♘f4 f6 19 g6 ♖xc3 20 ♕h7 mate.

(b) as above up to 12 ... c4!? 13 ♗c2 h6 14 f4 0–0–0! This game was played later. Having been mated on the kingside, was the NOVAG SUPER EXPERT trying to improve by playing its king to a safer area? 15 0–0 g5?! 16 fxg5 hxg5 17 ♘xg5 ♖df8 18 ♖f4 ♖h5 19 ♘h3 ♖fh8 20 ♖bf1. Black's play is "imaginative" but not sound, and the compensation is insufficient (1–0, 56).

3	...	e6
4	♗d3	c5
5	c3	♗d6

6	♗g3	0-0
7	♘bd2	♘c6
8	♘gf3	a6
9	a4!	

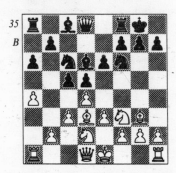

35
B

Against machines it is worth denying the clear plan which would follow on Black's achievement of the advance ... b5.

9	...	b6
10	0-0	♗xg3

Stronger is 10 ... ♗b7, since the text weakens Black's dark squares. However, NOVAG SUPER EXPERT wants to play ... ♗d7 (to attack White's a4 pawn?) rather than ... ♗b7, so this is a necessary preliminary.

11	hxg3	♗d7
12	♘e5	♘xe5

Otherwise f4 is very strong.

13	dxe5	♘e8
14	f4	c4?

This weakens d4.

15	♗c2	f6
16	♘f3	♗c6
17	♘d4	♕d7

18	♕h5	f5
19	g4	g6

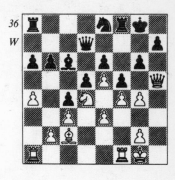

36
W

Black's position, with weak dark squares and a threatened king's wing, is highly critical, yet NOVAG SUPER EXPERT tried to defend this position against me no less than three times (!) in games well spaced out over the 59 total we contested. Does this mean that NOVAG SUPER EXPERT's castling queenside improvement in the 3 c3 game was a fluke, or does the machine have a stubborn streak?

20	♕h4	

Another game went: 20 ♕g5 ♘g7 21 ♖f3 fxg4 22 ♕xg4 ♘f5 23 ♗xf5 exf5 24 ♕g5 ♗xa4 25 ♔h2 b5 26 ♖h1 a5 27 ♖h3 ♖fe8 28 ♔g3 ♕g7 29 ♔f2 ♖a6 30 ♖g3 ♖f8 31 e6 ♖f6 32 ♘xf5! ♕f8 33 ♘d4 ♖d6 34 ♕e5 b4 35 ♖g5 bxc3 36 bxc3 ♖b6 37 ♕xd5 (1-0, 58).

20	...	♘g7
21	♖f3	

I also tried in a later game 21
gxf5 ♘xf5 22 ♗xf5 exf5 23 a5
bxa5 24 ♖xa5 ♛b7 25 ♖a2 ♖a7
26 e6 ♖e8 27 ♛f6 ♖f8 28 ♛e5
♖c8 29 ♖f3 ♖c7 30 ♖g3 ♖e7 31
♘xf5! ♖g7 32 ♘h6+ ♔h8 33 f5
♛b3 34 ♖a1 ♛xb2 35 ♖f1 ♗e8
36 f6 ♛b7 37 f7 ♛xf7 and 1–0.

	21	...	fxg4
	22	♛xg4	♖f7
	23	♖h3	♘f5

Exchange of White's bishop for
Black's knight is, of course strategic suicide but Black had to
block the radius of White's bishop.

	24	♗xf5	exf5
	25	♛g5	♖e8
	26	♔f2	♖g7
	27	a5!	

Further weakening Black's dark
squares and starting an attack on
both sides of the board.

	27	...	bxa5
	28	♖xa5	♖b8
	29	♖a2	♛c8
	30	♛f6	

Queen penetration is decisive.

	30	...	♖c7
	31	e6	♖cb7
	32	♘xf5!	*(37)*

If now 32 ... gxf5 33 ♖g3+
wins at once. Black has defended
ingeniously but the threats were
too much.

	32	...	♖xb2+
	33	♖xb2	♖xb2+
	34	♔g1	♖xg2+

Absolute 'desperation'.

37
B

	35	♔xg2	d4+
	36	♔h2	♛f8
	and 1–0		

(Times in minutes: 2.11/2.39)

Ray Keene–NOVAG SUPER EXPERT

Test Blitz Game, London, 1989

	1	d4	♘f6
	2	c4	g6
	3	♘c3	d5
	4	cxd5	♘xd5
	5	e4	♘xc3
	6	bxc3	♗g7
	7	♗c4	0–0
	8	♘e2	c5
	9	♗e3	

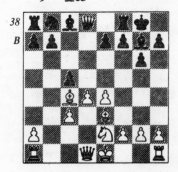

38
B

A sharp theoretical variation, popularised by many games between Karpov and Kasparov. I have never played this as either colour, but I decided to find out how much theory NOVAG SUPER EXPERT knew.

9	...	♘c6
10	0–0	cxd4
11	cxd4	♗g4
12	f3	♘a5
13	♗xf7+	

Karpov's speciality. The machine still did not slow down, firing out its moves instantly.

13	...	♖xf7
14	fxg4	♖xf1+
15	♔xf1	♛b6
16	♛d3	♛e6
17	h3!?	

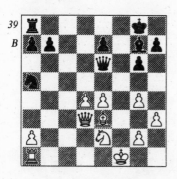

39
B

17 ♔g1 would transpose to Karpov–Kasparov (9), Seville 1987. There 17 ... ♛xg4 18 ♖f1 ♖c8 19 h3 ♛d7 20 d5 was better for White. But how bad can the text be? In any case, NOVAG

SUPER EXPERT's theoretical knowledge in fashionable lines looks outstanding.

17	...	♘c4
18	♗f2	♖f8
19	♔g1	♔h8

A useful precaution against checks or pins on the a2–g8 diagonal.

20	♖c1	♛f6
21	♗g3	b5
22	♔h2	a6
23	h4	

There are safer ways to proceed, but Karpov has won games by playing h4 and g5 to blot out the black bishop.

23	...	♛e6
24	g5	♛g4

It is typical of this machine to rush its pieces into the vicinity of the opposing king.

25	♘g1	♘d6
26	♖e1	

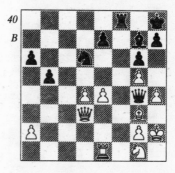

40
B

Now I thought that Black was dead. White has an extra pawn plus a solid position, with ♘f3 coming as the final consolidating nail in Black's coffin. However, Black now uncorks a remarkable resource.

| 26 | ... | ♖f4 |

I was really shocked by this, though on reflection it is probably the only chance to stay in the game.

| 27 | ♗xf4 | ♛xh4+ |
| 28 | ♛h3 | ♛xf4+ |

Of course not 28 ... ♛xe1 29 ♗xd6 exd6 30 ♛c8+ winning. As played, I still feel Black should lose, but the position is less clear than it was and time was running short.

29	♛g3	♛d2
30	♘f3	♛xa2
31	♛g4	♛f2
32	♛d7	♗f8
33	♛d8	♔g8
34	d5	♘c4
35	♛d7	♘d2!

41
W

Another beautiful riposte. White has been wasting far too much time with the queen over

the past 7 moves. I now decided to force a draw. In the seconds available I could not see a clear win.

36	♛e6+	♔h8
37	♛e5+	♔g8
38	♛e6+	½–½

Drawn by perpetual check. Black used 2.21 minutes over this game, less than half the time consumed by White. This was the NOVAG SUPER EXPERT's best game in the 59 long sequence which I played against it.

DEEP THOUGHT–Mike Valvo
Played by Computer Mail, December 1988 to March 1989

1	e4	e5
2	f4	d5
3	exd5	c6
4	♘c3	exf4
5	♘f3	♗d6
6	d4	♘e7
7	dxc6	♘bxc6
8	d5	♘b4
9	♗c4	0-0
10	a3	b5!
11	♗b3	

42
B

Up to here the position is known to theory, but at this point DEEP THOUGHT tries an improvement on 11 ♗xb5, which has been proved weak. It rejected 11 ♘xb5 on account of ... ♘bxd5 12 ♗xd5 ♘xd5 13 c4 ♖e8+ 14 ♔f1 ♗c5 15 ♕xd5 ♗f5 with a murderous attack.

11	...	♘a6
12	♘xb5	♕a5+
13	♘c3	♘c5
14	♗a2	

An ambitious move which seeks to cling to the extra pawn on d5 whilst simultaneously threatening b4 to fork Black's queen and knight.

Safer would have been 14 0–0 ♘xb3 15 cxb3 even though ... ♗b7 regains the pawn.

14	...	♗a6

Giving up a piece to prevent White from castling.

15	b4	♕c7
16	bxc5	

If instead 16 b5, then ♗xb5 17 ♘xb5 ♕a5+. At this point DEEP THOUGHT looked 19 single moves deep into Black's sacrifice but could not refute it. However, DEEP THOUGHT was unable to find anything better than taking the piece.

16	...	♖fe8
17	♘e2	♕xc5
18	c4	♘xd5
19	♕d4	

If 19 ♕xd5 ♖xe2+ 20 ♔d1 ♕xd5+ 21 cxd5 ♖xg2 with the plan of ... g5–g4.

19	...	♕xd4
20	♘xd4	♗c5
21	♔d2	

White has several alternatives here to break the pins but most fail to ... ♖e4.

21	...	♘e3
22	♔c3	♖ac8
23	♗b2	♘xg2
24	♖af1	♖cd8
25	♖hg1	♖e3+
26	♔d2	f3
27	♖xf3	

If 27 ♖xg2? either 27 ... ♖xe2+ or 27 ... fxe2.

27	...	♖xf3
28	♖xg2	♖h3

Not 28 ... ♗xa3? 29 ♔c2.

29	♔c1	g6

Preventing any ♖xg7+ tricks.

30	a4	♗b7
31	♖f2	♗a8

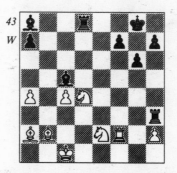

White is virtually in zugzwang. If instead, 31 ... ♗e4 32 ♗b1

♗xb1 33 ♔xb1 ♖d3 34 ♔c2 ♖xd4 35 ♘xd4 ♗xd4 36 ♗xd4 ♖xd4 37 ♔c3 and White has chances with the passed c-pawn.

	32	♗b1	♖b8
	33	♗a2	♖d3
	34	♖f4	♖d2!!

44
W

This brilliant move breaks the back of White's resistance.

	35	♔xd2	♖xb2+
	36	♘c2	♖xa2
	37	♘c3	♖b2
	38	♖f6	♔g7
	39	♖f1	

If 39 ♖a6 ♗b6 40 a5 ♗g1 and Black wins.

	39	...	f5
	40	♘d5	♗xd5
	41	cxd5	♖b3
	42	h4	♔f6
	43	♖e1	♖h3
	44	♖e6+	♔f7
	45	a5	♖xh4
	46	♖c6	♗b4+
	47	♘xb4	♖xb4
	48	♖c7+	♔f6

White resigns

If 49 ♖xh7 ♖d4+ 50 ♔e3 ♖xd5 51 ♖xa7 ♔g5 and Black's pawns promote, while the black rook will station itself on the a-file behind White's passed pawn to terminate its progress. Valvo said of this game: "The slow time rate paradoxically benefited the human player much more than the computer. The Computer thinks like a flashlight in the dark. What it sees it sees perfectly. What it does not see it cannot even make a poor guess at. The positional sacrifice of a piece in this game underscores this point. The only chance humans have against these tactical monsters is long term positional ideas. Tactical fire-fights are generally mistakes."

CRAY BLITZ–David Levy
1984

(Notes based on those by David Levy)

	1	e4	a6
	2	d4	g6

Taking the program out of its openings book at the earliest possible stage. This was part of our pre-match planning, designed to take advantage of the fact that programs do not "understand" the finer points of chess opening strategy. The program's next few moves are natural but stereotyped.

3	♘f3	♗g7
4	♘c3	

Possibly inaccurate. In our pre-match analysis we had considered 4 c3 to be best, supporting the d4 pawn and depriving Black of any queenside counter-play based on the thrust ... c5. However, we had expected CRAY BLITZ to play that move, which develops a minor piece.

4	...	b5
5	♗d3	♗b7
6	0-0	d6
7	♗f4	e6

Probably better is 7 ... ♘d7, when 8 e5 loses the pawn to 8 ... ♗xf3 9 ♕xf3 dxe5. After 7 ... ♘d7 Black will soon strike at White's pawn centre with ... c5.

8 e5

Part of Black's weird looking opening idea is to develop his knights on e7 and d7 and to meet the advance e5 with ... d5 (followed by an eventual ... c5) or the advance d5 with ... e5 (followed by an eventual ... f5). With the pawn centre locked, the program will find itself in the type of position it handles least well.

8	...	d5
9	b4!	

When the program played this move my first reaction was that it had to be a mistake, since it cedes Black control of the c4 square and creates long term prospects for

45
B

the g7 bishop along the h8–a1 diagonal. But on closer inspection I realised that CRAY BLITZ now had a clear positional advantage, partly because of the possibility of ♘f3–d2, ♘d2–b3 and ♘b3–c5 (or ♘b3–a5 in some positions).

9	...	♘d7
10	♕d2	♘e7?!

Better might have been 10 ... h6 first, and only then ... ♘e7.

11	a4!	c6

There are now three ways for White to handle the tension on the queenside:
(a) Maintain the tension by keeping the pawn on a4 and reserving all options.
(b) Closing the position with 12 a5 in order to kill any prospects of queenside play for Black. In reply to this move I would have played ... h6, followed by ... ♕c7, ... 0-0-0, ... g5, with a very strong kingside attack in the offing. The sceptical reader may well argue that while Black was putting this

plan into effect, White could well be marshalling its forces in preparation for a sacrificial attack on the queenside, but a computer program in 1984 would never have devised a plan in which material is sacrificed in return for long-term attacking prospects against my queenside. In other words, I could be almost certain that during the ten moves required to initiate my own attack the program would have sat and twiddled its registers.

(c)   Release the tension at once, and at the same time give Black's b7-bishop a new lease of life and leave White with a potentially vulnerable c-pawn on the half-open file. CRAY BLITZ chooses the third and weakest of these possibilities.

12   axb5?   cxb5
13   ♗h6   0-0

On 13 ... ♗xh6? 14 ♕xh6, Black has no way to save the h-pawn against the dual threats of ♕g7 and ♘g5.

14   ♗g5??

Wasting a tempo. White should probably have traded bishops on g7 in order to set up an attack on the black squares around my king.

14   ...   ♖e8
15   ♖a3!?

Another occasion on which my first reaction was that CRAY BLITZ was floundering, but the

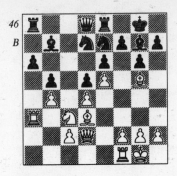

46
B

real point of this move lies not in any attempt to control the a-file but in the possibility of switching this rook to h3 as part of an assault on my king.

15   ...   ♘b6
16   ♘d1   ♘c4
17   ♗xc4   dxc4

Now that my b7 bishop has real scope, White must take care. 18 ♘e3 would allow 18 ... ♗xf3 19 gxf3 ♕b6, with a perfectly reasonable position for Black.

18   ♘b2?!

A strange square for the knight, and one on which it has no genuine prospects, but it is already difficult to suggest a good plan for White.

18   ...   ♕c7

Now CRAY BLITZ has the unenviable choice between trading on e7, thereby giving me a potentially won endgame due to possession of two bishops against two knights, or permitting my knight to jump into play on f5 and d5.

19   ♖fa1   ♖ec8

Now 20 ... c3 is a serious threat, and 20 ♗xe7 is too late (20 ... c3 21 ♗d6 cxd2 22 ♗xc7 ♖xc7 and 23 ... ♖xc2)

20   c3?

20 ♘d1 was forced, but it is easy to understand why CRAY BLITZ did not fear the ensuing continuation. Black can only capture on f3 at the cost of "losing" a pawn, which no materialistic computer program would ever sanction. An 11-ply search ending with 25 ♖xb5 would conclude that White was a pawn ahead, which is absolutely true but totally irrelevant!

20	...	♗xf3
21	gxf3	♘f5

Black cannot save both the knight and the a6-pawn.

22	♖xa6	♖xa6
23	♖xa6	♛b7
24	♖a5	♛xf3
25	♖xb5	

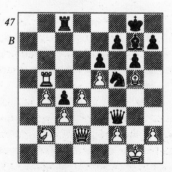

CRAY BLITZ has won its pawn but at what cost! Its kingside is full of holes and in the long term it will not be able to defend against the combined attack from my queen and knight.

Botvinnik once wrote that the chess player's greatest art lies in creating positions in which the normal relative values cease to exist. One can extrapolate from his assertion by saying that the art of defeating chess programs easily lies in creating positions where the program's evaluation function fails to account for the true relative values as perceived by a human chess master.

25   ...   h6

The spectators now expected 26 ♗f6, when 26 ... g5! is very strong. The program finds a better defence.

26   ♗f4   ♛h3!

Since 26 ... ♘h4 allows 27 ♔f1. I wanted to keep the white king under lock and key.

27	♗g3	h5
28	♖c5!	♖a8
29	♛c1??	

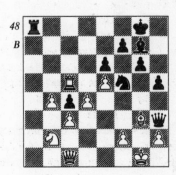

This move protects the back rank against incursion by my rook at a1, and prepares for ♕c1–f1, but the defence is inadequate. If the program had not been moving rather quickly it might have found 29 ♖a5!, when 29 … ♖a5? 30 bxa5, leaves White with a dangerous passed pawn, while after 29 … ♖f8 30 ♘xc4 ♗h6 31 ♕a2 h4 32 ♖a8 hxg3 33 hxg3, it is not exactly clear whether Black's extra bishop is more (or less) than a match for White's extra pawns. In a game against a computer I would expect to win with Black, but against a human player I would be very much concerned about the hordes of advancing pawns.

29   …   h4

After the game Danny Kopec pointed out the beautiful win 29 … ♗h6 30 ♕f1 ♘e3!! 31 fxe3 (if 31 ♕xh3 ♖a1+ forces mate) 31 … ♗xe3+ 32 ♗f2 ♕g4+ 33 ♔h1 ♕f3+ 34 ♔g1 ♗xf2+ 35 ♕xf2 ♖a1+ etc. My move is far less exciting but just as effective.

30   ♗f4   ♕f3
31   h3

The only way to prevent 31 … h3 without losing the bishop.

31   …   ♕xh3
32   ♖xc4   ♕f3

Echoing the threat of … h3 which this time cannot be stopped.

33   ♗h2

33 ♔f1 loses the queen to 33 … ♖a1! 34 ♕xa1 ♕h1+ and 35 … ♕xa1.

33   …   h3
34   ♕f1   ♖a1
35   ♘d1   ♖xd1

White resigns

8 World Champions Against the Computer

In October 1989 the long awaited clash took place between Gary Kasparov, the human World Champion, and DEEP THOUGHT, the supreme chess computer. Kasparov played from the New York Academy of Arts in Greenwich Village, while DEEP THOUGHT beamed its moves via an electronic link from its home base in Pittsburgh.

The general expectation was that Kasparov would win, but the manner of his eventual victory must have been disturbing for the machine's programmers. Although DEEP THOUGHT can examine positions at a rate of 750,000 per second, Kasparov swiftly detected in his pre-game investigation of DEEP THOUGHT's earlier games, that the mental mind was susceptible to strategic squeezes and tended to flounder in openings which were not a regular part of its repertoire.

Indeed, the champion ruthlessly exploited the insights he had gained into DEEP THOUGHT's prior body of games. The expert, playing through the two games which follow, will appreciate that there is no real clash of ideas, such as might occur in a game between two humans of reasonable strength, whatever the disparity in their ratings. Both of Kasparov's wins are in the nature of academic demonstrations in which the computer is only given the chance to react. The helpless shuffling of White's king around the 29th move of the first game underscores this point. Kasparov charitably predicted that DEEP THOUGHT would approach Grandmaster level within two to three years, but unless there is a huge improvement in strategic grasp, this remains optimistic. Further, as DEEP THOUGHT's games become more widely accessible, special preparation by Grandmaster opponents will certainly make the machine's task more difficult.

DEEP THOUGHT–Gary Kasparov
New York, 1989

1	e4	c5
2	c3	

This variation of the Sicilian is popular with computers, but Kasparov has seen DEEP THOUGHT play this before and was doubtless well prepared against it.

2	...	e6
3	d4	d5
4	exd5	exd5
5	♘f3	♗d6
6	♗e3	c4

Black's two strong bishops are working well together to contribute to the Champion's space advantage.

7	b3	cxb3
8	axb3	

DEEP THOUGHT has moved out of its "openings book".

8	...	♘e7
9	♘a3	♘bc6
10	♘b5	

This merely wastes time.

10	...	♗b8
11	♗d3	♗f5

DEEP THOUGHT should avoid the exchange of light squared bishops.

12	c4	

This weakens b4. DEEP THOUGHT had a bug in its castling code here and kept giving other moves priority, although it wanted to castle.

12	...	0–0
13	♖a4	♕d7
14	♘c3	♗c7
15	♗xf5	♕xf5
16	♘h4	♕d7
17	0–0	♖ad8
18	♖e1	♖fe8

DEEP THOUGHT assessed this position as favourable to White, but Black's control of the light squares gives him a tangible edge over the machine.

19	c5	♗a5
20	♕d3	a6
21	h3	♗xc3
22	♕xc3	♘f5
23	♘xf5	♕xf5

Black's rooks are strong, while White's rooks are badly placed.

24	♖a2	♖e6
25	♖ae2	♖de8
26	♕d2	f6
27	♕c3	

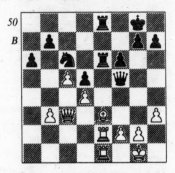

50
B

The computer still thought this position was equal, but White is strategically lost and cannot evolve any kind of active plan.

27	...	h5
28	b4	♖8e7
29	♔h1	g5
30	♔g1	g4
31	h4	♖e4
32	♕b2	♘a7
33	♕d2	♖4e6
34	♕c1	♘b5
35	♕d2	♘a3
36	♕d1	♔f7
37	♕b3	♘c4
38	♔h2	♖e4
39	g3	♕f3
40	b5	a5

Kasparov's passed a-pawn will prove to be the computer's downfall.

41	c6	f5

51
W

42	cxb7	♖xb7
43	♔g1	f4
44	gxf4	g3
45	♕d1	♖be7
46	b6	gxf2+
47	♖xf2	♕xd1
48	♖xd1	♖xe3
49	♖g2	♘xb6
50	♖g5	a4
51	♖xh5	a3
52	♖d2	♖e2

White resigns.

Gary Kasparov–DEEP THOUGHT
New York, 1989

1	d4	d5
2	c4	dxc4

DEEP THOUGHT's desire to hang on to the pawn will lead to trouble.

3	e4	♘c6

3 ... e5 is better.

4	♘f3	♗g4
5	d5	♘e5
6	♘c3	c6
7	♗f4	♘g6
8	♗e3	cxd5
9	exd5	♘e5

52
W

DEEP THOUGHT, like most computers, is keen to grab material, but this is ill-advised.

10	♕d4	♘xf3+
11	gxf3	♗xf3
12	♗xc4	♕d6

White was threatening 13 ♗b5+.

13	♘b5	♕f6
14	♕c5	♕b6

If 14 ... ♗xh1 15 ♘c7+ ♔d8 16 ♘xa8 and Black is helpless.

15	♕a3	e6 (53)
16	♘c7+	

Kasparov forces Black to surrender its queen, after which resistance is useless.

16	...	♕xc7
17	♗b5+	♕c6
18	♗xc6+	bxc6
19	♗c5	♗xc5

53
W

If 19 ... ♗xh1 20 ♗xf8, threatening 21 ♗xg7.

20	♕xf3	♗b4+
21	♔e2	cxd5
22	♕g4	♗e7
23	♖hc1	♔f8
24	♖c7	♗d6
25	♖b7	♘f6
26	♕a4	a5
27	♖c1	h6
28	♖c6	♘e8
29	b4	♗xh2
30	bxa5	♔g8
31	♕b4	♗d6
32	♖xd6	♘xd6
33	♖b8+	♖xb8
34	♕xb8+	♔h7
35	♕xd6	♖c8
36	a4	♖c4
37	♕d7	

Black resigns.

Anatoly Karpov–DEEP THOUGHT
Harvard University, 1990

1	e4	c6
2	d4	d5

3 ♘d2 g6

This is a surprise as White can now strengthen his centre with 4 c3, which would not have been possible if he had played 3 ♘c3 countered by 3 ... g6 — the "Gurgenidze Variation".

4 c3 ♗g7
5 e5

Karpov's fifth move marked the end of DEEP THOUGHT's openings "book". 5 e5 blocks the position and thus follows conventional anti-computer tactics, but it also concedes Black some counterplay based on the thrusts ... f6 and ... c5. If the former World Champion had opted for the more amorphous lines after 5 ♘gf3 he might well have given the machine more intractable problems, for example 5 ♘gf3 ♘h6 6 ♗d3 0-0 7 0-0 ♘d7 (7 ... f6 8 ♖e1 ♘f7 9 c4 is highly artificial for Black) 8 ♖e1 (it is premature to play 8 e5 ♖e8 9 h3 f6 10 exf6 exf6 =, Prasad–Skembris, Dubai Olympiad 1986) 8 ... ♖e8 9 h3 and White has the more flexible structure.

5 ... f6
6 f4 ♘h6
7 ♘gf3

White now has problems trying to co-ordinate his pieces. DEEP THOUGHT was, in fact, expecting 7 ♘df3, which is much more logical, with the intention of fol-

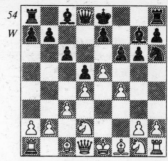

lowing up with ♗d3 and ♘e2.

7 ... 0-0
8 ♗e2

Karpov later said that he thought 8 ♗d3 was better, but he had underestimated the amount of counterplay now obtained by his opponent.

8 ... fxe5

DEEP THOUGHT now obtains active counterplay.

9 fxe5 c5

Based on 10 dxc5 ♘g4 with some advantage to Black.

10 ♘b3 cxd4
11 cxd4 ♘c6
12 0-0 ♕b6
13 ♔h1

In this position White has some problems. The pawn on d4 is a major liability, his pieces are not well placed and are not working together well.

13   ...   a5
14   a4

14 ♘c5 could be best here, when White can reposition his knight with ♘c5–a4–c3.

14   ...   ♗f5
15   ♗g5

15 ♘c5 would surely be better. Now the b-pawn is unprotected and the bishop on g5 is under attack.

15   ...   ♗e4

Black is at least equal now, possibly even better.

16   ♘c5

If Black plays correctly this would not be best. Black has put great pressure on the white centre and White should not allow 16 ... ♘f5. But Karpov's play is based on knowledge of the well-known materialism of computers. Few machines could resist playing Black's next move!

16   ...   ♕xb2

The lure of an easily edible pawn has proved too much. In the process DEEP THOUGHT overlooked the exchange sacrifice 16 ... ♘f5, when after 17 ♘d7 ♕xb2 18 ♘xf8 ♘fxd4 White's position hangs on threads. Black is temporarily a rook down, but threatens

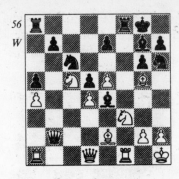

... ♘xe2 and ... ♘b3, as well as recapturing the knight on f8.

17   ♘xe4

It would be more appropriate to follow a quieter course with 17 ♘e6 in order to trade off Black's valuable bishop.

17   ...   dxe4
18   ♖b1   ♕a3

This is forced. 18 ... ♕c3 loses the queen to 19 ♖b3, while 18 ... ♕a2 runs into 19 ♘d2.

19   ♗c1   ♕c3
20   ♗d2   ♕a3
21   ♗c1   ♕c3
22   ♖b3

Karpov was short of time and could think while his opponent's time was running. Unlike its human opponent the computer does not remember what it thought about before and had to rethink the position each time. When asked why DEEP THOUGHT took so long for seemingly obvious moves, programmer Murray Campbell says that the program thinks the same amount of time for every move.

22	...	♛a1
23	♗c4+	♚h8

The ensuing liquidation looks dramatic, but ends in equality.

24	♗xh6	♛xd1
25	♗xg7+	♚xg7
26	♖xd1	exf3
27	gxf3	♖a7

According to Karpov this was the only choice, but it raised a laugh amongst the audience when it appeared on the screen.

28	♗d5	♖d8
29	♖b5	♖a6

The computer is very resourceful. DEEP THOUGHT now threatens 30 ... ♘a7 31 ♗xb7 ♘xb5 32 ♗xa6 ♖xd4 with equality.

30	♗c4	♖a7
31	♗d5	♖a6
32	♖c5	♖d7

32 ... ♖b6 immediately looks more accurate.

33	♚g2	♖b6
34	♗xc6	bxc6
35	♚f2	

Risky, but Karpov still wants to win. Objectively he should have played 35 ♖xa5!

35	...	♖d5!
36	♖xd5	cxd5
37	♖c1	♖b4
38	♚e3	♖xa4

DEEP THOUGHT could now have secured a draw with 38 ... ♖b3+ 39 ♚e2 ♖b4 when White cannot afford to give up his d-pawn.

39	♖c5	e6
40	♖c7+	♚g8
41	♖e7	♖a3+
42	♚f4	♖d3
43	♖xe6	♖xd4+
44	♚g5	♚f7
45	♖a6	

Here there was an easy draw after 45 ... h6+ 46 ♚xh6 ♖h4+ 47 ♚g5 ♖h5+ 48 ♚f4 ♖f5+ and ... ♖xe5, but the computer had

thought that it stood better since
move 35.

45	...	a4
46	f4	h6+
47	♔g4	♖c4

In the post mortem Karpov said
he thought 47 ... g5 could still
draw, but the computer still
thought it was up a pawn.

48	h4	♖d4
49	♖f6+	♔g7
50	♖a6	♔f7
51	h5	

DEEP THOUGHT finally
realised here that it was worse.

51	...	gxh5+
52	♔f5!	♔g7
53	♖a7+	♔f8
54	e6	♖e4

To prevent 55 ♔e5–d6.

| 55 | ♖d7 | ♖c4 |
| 56 | ♖xd5 | h4 |

Now there is a pawn race, but
Karpov has calculated that his
centralised forces will outrun his
opponent's pawns.

57	♖d3	♔e7
58	♖d7+	♔f8
59	♖h7	h5
60	♔e5	h3
61	f5	♔g8
62	♖xh5	a3
63	♖xh3	a2
64	♖a3	♖c5+
65	♔f6	

The programmers had decided
in advance to resign the game if
the machine saw that White would
queen a pawn. This game shows
how dangerous the metal minds
are becoming!

9 Taming the Monster

Since the late 18th century, when Baron Wolfgang von Kempelen, Aulic Councillor to the Imperial Court of Vienna, constructed his chess playing automaton "The Turk", there has been endless fascination with the notion of chess playing machines. Napoleon fell prey to this desire to test his own mental powers against a mechanical brain when he challenged the automaton at Schönbrunn Castle in Vienna 1809. That game inspired a similar incident in Raymond Bernard's epic silent film *Le Joueur d'Echecs* of 1927 which depicts a scene where The Turk faces the Russian Empress Catherine the Great. Indeed, Napoleon's stepson Eugène de Beauharnais (1781–1824) purchased The Turk in 1811 for the then enormous sum of 30,000 francs. Most of Napoleon's games that have come down to us we regard as apocryphal, being shallow brilliancies in which the emperor's mental faculties on the sixty-four squares receive un-

due credit from posthumous sycophants. In the following game, though, Napoleon's moves are so bad as to be plausible.

Napoleon Bonaparte–Automaton (The Turk)
Schönbrunn, 1809

1 e4 e5 2 ♗c4 ♘c6 3 ♕f3 ♘f6 4 ♘e2 ♗c5 5 a3 d6 6 0–0 ♗g4 7 ♕d3 ♘h5 8 h3 ♗xe2 9 ♕xe2 ♘f4 10 ♕e1 ♘d4 11 ♗b3 ♘xh3+

61
W

12 ♔h2 ♕h4 13 g3 ♘f3+ 14 ♔g2 ♘xe1+ 15 ♖xe1 ♕g4 16 d3 ♗xf2 17 ♖h1 ♕xg3+ 18 ♔f1 ♗d4 19

♔e2 ♕g2+ 20 ♔d1 ♕xh1+ 21 ♔d2 ♕g2+ 22 ♔e1 ♘g1 23 ♘c3 ♗xc3+ 24 bxc3 ♕e2 Mate. A very one-sided game!

Of course, The Turk was not a true computer but a mechanical device in which a human player (in this case reputedly Allgaier, Vienna's strongest player of the day) was ingeniously concealed.

In 1989, experts on genuine chess playing computers were confidently predicting that within five years the best machines would be able to outplay the human World Champion. So far, thankfully, grandmasters are still warding off the challenge, in spite of the fact that IBM is enthusiastically funding the upgrading of the world's most dangerous chess playing computer DEEP THOUGHT. DEEP THOUGHT Mk 1 could see a staggering 750,000 chess positions per second, while DEEP THOUGHT Mk 2, with IBM's assistance, has pushed this up to an amazing ten million. In order to defeat Kasparov, their goal is the visualisation of a barely credible one billion positions per second, though evidently there would be some technical difficulties in achieving this.

Why should scientists be so anxious to concentrate so much energy and so many resources on chess? A recent explanation advanced by various experts in the field is that chess is to artificial intelligence what Drosophilia Melanogaster (the fruit fly) is to genetic biology. It is well-known that the fruit fly is an outstanding subject for empirical experiments. They need little food, you can enclose thousands of them in a glass and new generations grow in a couple of days. Chess, so the argument runs, is the intelligence game par excellence in which complex decision situations can be studied and replicated on the computer.

Conventional wisdom dictates that the correct way to tackle a chess computer is by a quiet Fabian strategy. The following game, submitted by a reader in Vienna, against one of the strongest commercial machines conforms to this conventional wisdom, but the victory by the German grandmaster Wahls against DEEP THOUGHT Mk 2 also shows that humans need not yet abandon overt aggression when facing their electronic opponents.

Dr. Marcel Stein–MEPHISTO LYON
Vienna, 1991

1 ♘f3 d5 2 d4 c5 3 dxc5 e6 4 ♗f4 ♗xc5 5 e3 ♘c6 6 ♗e2 ♘ge7 7 a3 0–0 8 b4 ♗d6 9 ♗xd6 ♕xd6

10 0–0 a5 11 b5 ♘e5 12 c4 b6 13
cxd5 ♘xd5 14 ♘c3 ♗b7 15 ♘xd5
exd5 16 ♘xe5 ♕xe5 17 ♖c1 ♖fc8
18 ♕d2 ♖c5 19 ♖xc5 bxc5 20
♗f3 c4 21 ♖c1 h6 22 a4 ♔f8 23
h3 g5 24 ♔f1 ♔g7 25 ♕c3

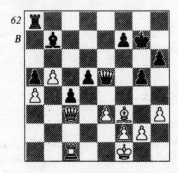

62
B

25 ... ♕xc3 26 ♖xc3 ♖c8 27 ♔e2
♔f6 28 ♔d2 ♔e5 29 ♖c1 f5 30
♔c3 f4 31 exf4+ gxf4 32 ♖e1+
♔d6 33 ♗g4 ♖c7 34 ♔d4 ♖e7
35 ♖xe7 ♔xe7 36 g3 fxg3 37 fxg3
♔d6 38 h4 ♗a8 39 ♗f5 ♗b7 40
g4 ♔e7 41 g5 hxg5 42 hxg5 ♔e8
43 g6 ♔f8 44 ♗d7 ♔e7 45 ♗c6
Black resigns.

In some desperation, having
suffered several defeats, Dr. Stein
rang Ray Keene for general advice
on how to defeat his new computer
(one of the strongest commercial
models) while the authors were
engaged in writing this book. The
advice, based on the principles
expounded in this volume, certainly paid off!

DEEP THOUGHT Mk 2–
Matthias Wahls
Hanover, 1991

1	d4	d6
2	c4	g6
3	♘c3	♗g7
4	e4	♘f6
5	f3	

Wahls, commenting on this
game himself, has a rather amus-
ing note here in which, perhaps
unconsciously, he ascribes an-
thropomorphic qualities to the
computer. Wahls wrote: "This
position could not be more theoretical. Several books have been
written about the Sämisch variation of the King's Indian and
thousands of important games
have been played with it. Suddenly
I found myself facing a giant openings databank. Also, it occurred
to me that DEEP THOUGHT
had been active as a commentator
during the World Championship
match and must therefore have
been fully conversant with the
Sämisch." (!)

5	...	0–0
6	♗e3	e5
7	♘ge2	c6
8	♕d2	♘bd7
9	d5	

Normal is 9 0–0–0 a6 10 ♔b1
b5 11 ♘c1 ♖e8 with both sides
maintaining the tension. After the
advance of the text one might
have expected 9 ... c5 to keep the

position a closed strategic one, in which computers are traditionally less adept. Wahls boldly opens up the game and invites a tactical mêlée.

9	...	cxd5
10	♘xd5	

After 10 cxd5 a6 we would have transposed to a normal position. One example of play (after 10 cxd5 a6) is 11 g4 h5 12 h3 ♘h7 13 0-0-0 h4 14 ♔b1 ♗f6 15 ♘c1 ♗g5 16 ♘b3 ♔g7 17 ♖c1 b6 18 ♗e2 ♘c5 19 ♘xc5 bxc5 20 ♘d1 ♗d7 21 ♖c3 ♗b5 22 ♖a3 ♕f6 23 ♕e1 ♖ab8 24 ♗xg5 ♘xg5 25 ♘e3 ♖h8 26 ♘g2 ♖b7 27 ♗xb5 ♖xb5 28 ♘xh4 ♖hb8 29 ♖h2 ♖8b6 30 ♕e3 ♘xe4 31 ♘f5+ gxf5 32 fxe4 f4 33 ♕e1 ♖b4 34 ♖f3 ♕g6 35 ♖e2 ♖xe4 36 ♔a1 ♖bb4 37 a3 ♖bd4 38 ♖f1 ♖xe2 39 ♕xe2 ♕d3 40 ♕g2 ♕b3 41 ♕e2 c4 42 ♖c1 c3 0–1 Gunawan–Maki, Thessaloniki Olympiad 1988. DEEP THOUGHT's move, recapturing with the piece on d5, is actually quite logical for a computer, speculating on the potential weakness of Black's backward pawn on d6. Many years of experience have taught human players that the d6 pawn tends to be considerably less vulnerable than would at first appear, but this kind of long range subtlety is difficult for a brute force computer to grasp.

10	...	♘xd5
11	♕xd5	♘b6

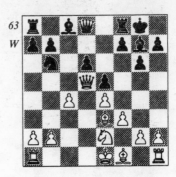

63
W

12	♕b5	♗h6!

A standard manoeuvre to activate Black's most passive piece. After 13 ♗xh6 ♕h4+ 14 ♘g3 ♕xh6 White would be fearfully weak on the dark squares.

13	♗f2	♗e6
14	♘c3	♕c7
15	b3	

It is possible to play 15 ♘d5, but after 15 ... ♗xd5 DEEP THOUGHT would be obliged to recapture with a pawn, thus eliminating its pressure against d6. The hyper-logical machine is naturally reluctant to do this.

15	...	♘d7
16	♕b4	a6
17	♖d1	♖fc8

DEEP THOUGHT would probably have been planning to capture the d-pawn at last, but the pawn is poisoned, for example 18 ♖xd6? ♗f8 or 18 ♕xd6 ♕a5 19

64
W

| 20 | ... | bxa4 |
| 21 | ♕xd6 | |

If 21 ♕xa4 ♘b6 22 ♗xb6 ♕xb6 leaves White wrecked on the dark squares.

| 21 | ... | ♕b7!! |

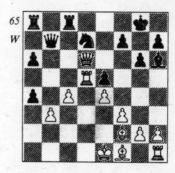

65
W

b4 ♕a3 or 19 ♕d3 b5. In both cases White is being rolled up on the queenside.

| 18 | ♘d5 | ♗xd5 |
| 19 | ♖xd5 | |

Absolutely consistent, in that White maintains its pressure against d6. Black's next move was based more on general principles than calculation. There has to be something when White's kingside army is asleep and White's king is still stuck in the centre.

| 19 | ... | b5 |
| 20 | a4? | |

The computer knows no fear. This can sometimes be an advantage but in this case is an absolute disadvantage. With White's development so retarded only a machine would think of intensifying the attack against Black's queenside and opening up lines in the very sector where Black has all the play. The last chance to get a playable position was 20 ♗e2.

DEEP THOUGHT is a great materialist and possibly did not devote enough attention to this move which, again, was played very much on instinct. Certainly it rapidly finishes the game, which is ironic when the computer is looking at 10 million positions per second while the human brain can scarcely be looking at more than one or two.

22 bxa4

Hopeless is 22 ♕xd7 ♕b4+ 23 ♔e2 axb3.

22	...	♗f8
23	♕xd7	♕b4+
24	♖d2	

This loses in banal fashion but if 24 ♔e2 ♕xc4+ 25 ♔e3 ♕c1+ 26 ♔e2 ♗b4 wins or 24 ♔d1

♛b3+ 25 ♔d2 ♛b2+ 26 ♔e3
♛c1+ 27 ♔e2 ♛xc4+ 28 ♔d1
♛c1+ 29 ♔e2 ♝b4 transposes
into the previous win.

| 24 | ... | ♖d8 |

66
W

25	♛xd8	♖xd8
26	♝e3	♝c5
27	♝g5	♖d6
28	♔e2	♖xd2+
		0–1

Study Material

The following games are the others
played by DEEP THOUGHT
Mk 2 at the tournament in Hanover.

Grünberg–DEEP THOUGHT
Hanover, 1991

1 d4 d5 2 c4 dxc4 3 ♘f3 a6 4 e4
b5 5 a4 ♝b7 6 axb5 axb5 7 ♖xa8
♝xa8 8 ♘c3 c6 9 ♝e2 e6 10
0–0 ♘d7 11 e5 ♘e7 12 ♝g5 ♛b8
13 ♘e4 ♘d5 14 ♛c2 h6 15 ♝h4
c5 16 ♖a1 cxd4 17 ♘xd4 ♘b4

18 ♖xa8 ♛xa8 19 ♘xb5 ♘xe5
20 ♛d1 ♘d5 21 ♘ec3

67
B

21 ... ♔d7 22 ♝g3 ♘d3 23 b3
♘xc3 24 ♘xc3 ♛a5 25 ♝xd3
cxd3 26 ♛xd3+ ♔e8 27 h3 ♝b4
28 ♘b5 ♔f8 29 ♔h2 ♔g8 30
♘c7 h5 31 h4 ♖h6 32 ♛d8+ ♔h7
33 ♛d3+ ♖g6 34 ♘b5 ♝e7 35 f3
♝b4 36 ♘d6 ♝e1 37 ♝xe1 ♛xe1
38 ♘e4 ♛xh4+ 39 ♔g1 ♛e1+ 40
♛f1 ♛e3+ 41 ♛f2 ♛xb3 42 ♛h4
♛b6+ 43 ♘f2 ♛b1+ 44 ♔h2 ♛e1
45 g4 ♛f1 46 ♔g3 ♛g1+ 47 ♔h3
f5 0–1

It is very risky to essay a dubious gambit against any computer!

DEEP THOUGHT–Bischoff
Hanover, 1991

1 d4 ♘f6 2 c4 e6 3 ♘c3 ♝b4 4
♛c2 d6 5 ♝g5 ♘bd7 6 e3 c5 7
♘f3 ♛a5 8 ♝d3 cxd4 9 exd4
♝xc3+ 10 bxc3 ♛c7 11 0–0 0–0
12 ♖fe1 b6 13 ♘d2 ♝b7 14 f3
♖fe8 15 ♝h4 h6 16 ♖e3 ♖ac8 17
♛b3 ♘h5 18 ♛a3 ♘df6 19 ♝c2
♖ed8

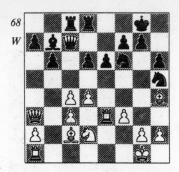

68
W

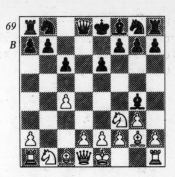

69
B

20 ♘e4 ♗xe4 21 fxe4 e5 22 ♗d3
♖e8 23 ♖ae1 ♘h7 24 ♗e2 ♘f4
25 ♗g4 ♖a8 26 ♕a4 ♘g6 27 ♗d7
♖f8 28 ♗g3 ♖fd8 29 ♗g4 ♘hf8
30 ♖f1 ♖e8 31 ♖ef3 ♖e7 32 ♗f5
♕b7 33 ♕b4 ♕c6 34 ♕b5 ♕xb5
35 cxb5 ♖c7 36 ♖e3 ♖e8 37 ♔h1
f6 38 ♖d3 ♔f7 39 ♗g4 ♔e7 40
♖fd1 ♖b8 41 ♗f5 ♘h8 42 ♗e1
h5 43 ♔g1 g6 44 ♗h3 ♘f7 45
♗d2 ♖bb7 46 ♖f1 ♖c4 47 a3
♖bc7 48 g4 h4 49 ♗g2 g5 50 ♖b1
♘e6 51 d5 ♘f4 52 ♖e3 ♖a4 53
♖b3 ♘d8 54 ♗f1 ♘b7 55 c4 ♘c5
56 ♖b2 a6 57 bxa6 ♖xa6 58 ♗b4
♘g6 59 ♔h1 ½–½

Lobron–DEEP THOUGHT
Hanover, 1991

1 ♘f3 d5 2 g3 c6 3 ♗g2 ♗g4 4
c4 e6 5 b3 dxc4 6 bxc4 *(69)*
6 ... ♘d7 7 ♗b2 ♕b6 8 ♕c2
♘gf6 9 0–0 ♗d6 10 d3 0–0 11
♘bd2 e5 12 ♖ab1 ♕a6 13 h3 ♗e6
14 ♘g5 ♗f5 15 ♗c3 ♘c5 16 e4
♗g6 17 f4 exf4 18 gxf4 ♘a4 19

♗a1 ♘d7 20 e5 ♗c5+ 21 ♔h2
♖e3 22 ♘ge4 ♗xd2 23 ♘xd2
♗f5 24 ♗e4 ♗xe4 25 ♘xe4
♘ac5 26 ♘d6 b6 27 ♖g1 g6 28 f5
♘b7 29 ♘e4 ♕a3 30 ♕d2 ♘bc5
31 ♕h6 ♕xa2+ 32 ♖g2 1–0

Quiet strategic opening play as
recommended in this book. Note
that Black early on mistakenly
trades a centre pawn for a wing
pawn, as in many of David Levy's
wins v computers which we have
earlier cited.

DEEP THOUGHT–Bönsch
Hanover, 1991

1 d4 ♘f6 2 c4 e6 3 ♘c3 d5 4 ♗g5
♗e7 5 ♘f3 h6 6 ♗xf6 ♗xf6 7
e3 0–0 8 ♕d2 a6 9 ♗e2 ♘c6 10
0–0 dxc4 11 ♗xc4 e5 12 d5 ♘e7
13 ♘e4 ♘f5 14 ♕c3 ♖e8 15 ♗b3
♘d6 16 ♘xf6+ ♕xf6 17 ♕xc7
♗g4 18 ♘d2 ♖ac8 19 ♕b6 e4 20
♖ab1 ♕g6 21 ♔h1 ♗e2 22 ♖fe1
♗d3 23 ♖bd1 ♖e5 24 f4 ♖h5 25
♔g1 ♖h4 26 ♘b1 ♗xb1 27 ♖xb1

⊡g4 28 ⊡e2 ♕f6 29 ♝d1 ⊡g6 30
⊡c2 ⊡xc2 31 ♝xc2 ♕f5 32 ♕d4
♕g4 33 g3 h5 34 ♝xe4 f5 35 ♝d3
h4 36 ♚g2 ♞e4 37 ♕c4

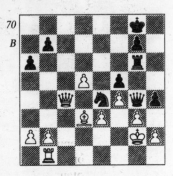

37 ... ♞xg3 38 h3 ♕h5 39 ♚f2
♚h7 40 ♕b4 a5 41 ♕e7 ♕h6 42
♕xb7 ⊡d6 43 ♕b5 ♕g6 44 ♕c5
⊡b6 45 b3 ♞h1+ 46 ♚e1 ⊡f6 47
♕xa5 ♕g2 48 ♕c5 ♞g3 49 d6 ♞e4
50 ♝xe4 ♕xe4 51 ⊡c1 ⊡g6 52
♚d2 ⊡g2+ 53 ♚c3 ⊡e2 54 d7
⊡xe3+ 55 ♚b2 ⊡d3 56 ♕f2 ♕e7
57 ⊡c7 ⊡xh3 58 ♕d2 ♕f6+ 59
♚b1 ⊡h1+ 60 ♚c2 ♕a1 61
d8(♕) ♕xa2+ 62 ♚c3 ♕a5+ 63
♚c4 ♕a6+ 64 ♚c5 ♕a3+ 65 b4
⊡c1+ 66 ♚b5 1-0

Black should have played 37 ...
h3+!, which wins.

Unzicker–DEEP THOUGHT
Hanover, 1991

1 ♞f3 d5 2 c4 dxc4 3 e3 c5 4 ♝xc4
e6 5 0-0 a6 6 b3 b5 7 ♝e2 ♝b7
8 ♝b2 ♞d7 9 a4 ♕b6 10 axb5
axb5 11 ⊡xa8+ ♝xa8 12 ♞a3

♝c6 13 d4 ♞gf6 14 dxc5 ♝xc5
15 ♞d4 ♝xd4 16 ♕xd4 b4 17 ♞c2
♕xd4 18 ♝xd4 ♞d5

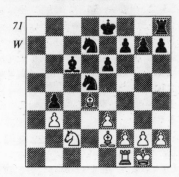

19 f3 e5 20 ♝b2 0-0 21 e4 ♞f4
22 ♝c4 ⊡b8 23 ⊡d1 ♞g6 24 ⊡d6
♞e7 25 ♝c1 ♞f6 26 ♝g5 ♝e8
27 ♝xf6 gxf6 28 ⊡xf6 ♚g7 29
⊡d6 ♞c6 30 ♝d5 ♞e7 31 ♝c4
♞c6 32 ♚f1 h5 33 h4 ♞e7 34
♚e1 ♞c6 35 ♚d2 f6 36 ♝d5
♞e7 37 ♞e3 ♝f7 38 ♝xf7 ♚xf7
39 ⊡a6 ⊡b7 40 ♞c4 ♞c8 41 ⊡c6
♞a7 42 ♞d6+ ♚e6 43 ⊡a6 ⊡d7
44 ♚e2 ⊡xd6 45 ⊡xa7 ⊡b6

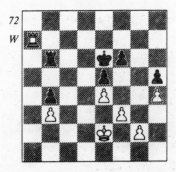

46 ♖c7 ♖b8 47 ♖c6+ ♔e7 48
♖c4 ♔f7 49 ♔f2 ♔g6 50 ♔g3
♖b6 51 ♔h3 ♔g7 52 ♖c5 ♖d6
53 ♖c4 ♖b6 54 g4 ♔h6 55 ♔g3
♔g6 56 ♖c5 hxg4 57 ♔xg4 ♔g7
58 ♔f5 ♖d6 59 ♖c7+ ♔h6 60
♖f7 ♖d3 61 ♖xf6+ ♔h5 62
♔xe5 ♔xh4 63 f4 ♖xb3 64 ♖b6
♖b1 65 f5 ♔g5 66 ♔e6 ♖f1 67
♖xb4 ♖a1 68 ♖d4 ♖a8 69 f6
1–0.

Once again the computer suffers
by surrendering a centre pawn
for a flank pawn. Quiet strategic
strangulation by the human
Grandmaster eventually triumphs.

Tischbierek–DEEP THOUGHT
Hanover, 1991

1 e4 c5 2 ♘c3 ♘c6 3 ♘ge2 e5 4
♘d5 d6 5 ♘ec3 ♘ge7 6 ♗c4 ♘xd5
7 ♗xd5 ♗e7 8 d3 ♘d4 9 0-0
♗h4 10 f4 0-0 11 f5 ♖b8 12 a4
♗d7 13 g3 ♗g5 14 ♖f2 ♗xc1
15 ♕xc1 ♗c6 16 f6 *(73)*
16 ... gxf6 17 ♕h6 ♕b6 18 ♕xf6

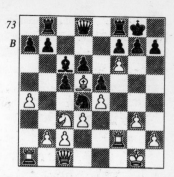

♗e8 19 ♖af1 ♕xb2 20 ♕g5+
♔h8 21 ♘d1 ♕b4 22 c3 ♕a3 1–0

Unorthodox opening play wins
quickly. The computer under-
estimates the potential concen-
tration of White forces against its
king. The computer has no natural
sense of danger in this respect.

DEEP THOUGHT's games
from Hanover show that even the
very best that modern technology
can offer does not yet dominate
the world of serious, well-prepared
Masters and Grandmasters. As
the reader studies these games,
some of the computer's long-term
weaknesses stand exposed.

Crosstable of Hanover Tournament

			1	2	3	4	5	6	7	8	
1	M. Wahls	2560	*	0	½	½	1	1	1	1	5
2	U. Bönsch	2535	1	*	1	½	½	½	0	1	4½
3	E. Lobron	2545	½	0	*	1	½	1	1	½	4½
4	K. Bischoff	2495	½	½	0	*	½	1	½	½	3½
5	H. Grünberg	2485	0	½	½	½	*	½	0	1	3
6	R. Tischbierek	2500	0	½	0	0	½	*	1	1	3
7	DEEP THOUGHT	(2410)	0	1	0	½	1	0	*	0	2½
8	W. Unzicker	2480	0	0	½	½	0	0	1	*	2

Finally, the following instructive games were played by the leading computers in the chess section at the first Computer Olympiad organised by David Levy and Raymond Keene held in London in August 1989.

FIDELITY–MEPHISTO
(Notes by RDK)
1st Computer Olympiad, 1989

1	e4	c6
2	d4	d5

MEPHISTO has chosen the ultrasolid Caro–Kann Defence. White's natural 3rd move is 3 ♘c3 but 3 ♘d2 is fashionable, for no particular reason that I can discern, therefore it must form part of FIDELITY's openings book.

3	♘d2	dxe4
4	♘xe4	♗f5

The Classical Variation, the favourite of Capablanca, World Champion from 1921–27.

5	♘g3	♗g6
6	h4	h6
7	h5	♗h7
8	♘f3	♘d7
9	♗d3	♗xd3
10	♕xd3	♕c7
11	♗d2	e6
12	♕e2	♘gf6
13	0–0–0	c5
14	c4	0–0–0
15	♘e5	♘b6

If 15 ... ♘xe5 16 dxe5 ♘d7 17 f4 gives White a very useful space advantage. Therefore Black maintains the tension in the centre.

16	♗f4	♗d6

To parry White's threat of ♘g6.

17	♔b1	♘bd7

The knight returns to challenge White's outpost on e5 now that Black's 16th move has prevented any discovered attacks against the black queen.

18	♘xd7	♖xd7
19	♗xd6	♖xd6
20	dxc5	♕xc5
21	♖xd6	♕xd6
22	♖d1	♕c6
23	f4	

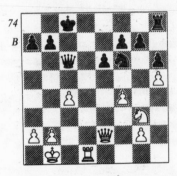

74
B

This move is somewhat dubious since it weakens White's pawns, however, White had to find some way of defending the pawn on g2 from attack by the black queen and after 23 f3, which is more solid, FIDELITY probably feared 23 ... ♕c5, attacking the white h-pawn.

23	...	♖d8
24	♖xd8+	♔xd8
25	b3	♕c5

The position might look drawish but as so often in the Caro–Kann, mass simplification tends to favour Black. Here Black's king is more secure and White's pawns are more scattered. So what was White's error? Probably 14 c4 and 15 ♘e5 just do not go together.

26	♕f3	♔c8
27	♔b2	♔b8

A curious waiting move which I do not fully understand.

28	♔b1

White is also at a loss for anything to do. If he waits with 28 ♔c2 then 28 ... ♘d5 29 ♘e4 ♘b4+ is annoying, since Black's knight has entered the attack. In place of 28 ♔b1, 28 a4 might be worth consideration. It further weakens White's queenside, but, on the other hand, it creates some air for the white king, viz the a2 square.

28	...	♕g1+
29	♔c2

I do not understand why this is preferred to 29 ♔b2, which keeps black's queen out of a1. Invasion now promptly occurs.

29	...	♕a1
30	a4	♕a2+
31	♔c3	♕b1
32	♕e3	b6
33	♕e5+	♔b7

34	♕e3	♔a6
35	♔b4	♕c2

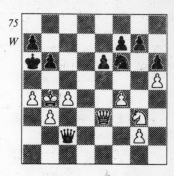

75
W

If now 36 ♕f3 (to defend g2) then 36 ... ♘d5+!! 37 cxd5 ♕c5 checkmate. Alternatively 36 ♕f3 ♘d5+!! 37 ♔a3 ♕c1+ 38 ♔a2 ♘b4 checkmate. In order to avoid this Mephistophelian trap, White must surrender a vital pawn.

36	♕e2	♕xe2

Absolutely not 36 ... ♘d5+ now since 37 cxd5 is discovered check.

37	♘xe2	♘xh5
38	♔c3	♔a5?

This ending should be an easy win for Black with his extra pawn and more compact position. However, the text move is completely ridiculous, only a computer would play it. There is no point at all in putting the king on this square. Black should win easily, re-centralising his king by means of 38 ... ♔b7.

39	♘d4!

White's best chance, activating his knight and speculating on the suddenly dangerous position of the black king.

39	...	♘xf4
40	♘c6+	♔a6
41	♘d8	f5
42	b4	b5

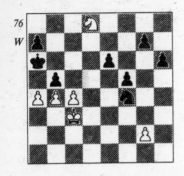

76
W

Disaster has struck. Due to Black's idiotic 38th move, White is now threatening 43 b5+ ♔a5 44 ♔b3 followed by checkmate on b7 or c6. In order to play for a win, Black must give up a vital pawn. He could, of course, play for a draw instead with 42 ... ♘e2+.

43	cxb5+	♔b6
44	♔c4	♔c7
45	♘c6	♘xg2

If instead 45 ... ♔b6 46 a5+ or 45 ... ♔b7 46 ♘d8+. The game now becomes a wild and incalculable race of passed pawns on opposite wings.

| 46 | ♘xa7 | f4 |

| 47 | ♘c6 | ♔d6 |

To prevent White from playing ♔c5 and b6+.

| 48 | ♔d3 | ♘e3 |

This knight scurries back to cope with the advance of White's queenside pawns. Protection of e3 for this purpose was one point of Black's 46th move.

| 49 | a5 | ♘d5 |
| 50 | a6 | g5 |

Understandably, Black wants to promote his passed pawns as quickly as possible. However, two improvements are available here. One would be 50 ... h5, trying to promote the pawn which is farthest distant from the white king. The other would be the defensive precaution 50 ... ♔c7, to meet 51 a7 with 51 ... ♔b7. As played, Black becomes locked into a defensive formation with his knight pinned down on b6 and later driven to a8.

51	a7	♘b6
52	♘a5	♔c7
53	♘c4	♘a8
54	b6+	♔b7
55	♔e4	h5

What a transformation has come over the position as a result of Black's incautious 50th move. By force, Black's king and knight have been driven onto the most clumsy squares and White is now in a position to decimate the army of Black's kingside pawns, which

had earlier seemed so overwhelming.

56	♞d6+	♚xb6
57	♞f7	g4
58	♚xf4	♚xa7
59	♞g5	♞c7
60	♞e4	

More accurate is the immediate 60 ♚g3–h4.

| 60 | ... | ♞d5+ |
| 61 | ♚g5 | e5 |

Suddenly the horrible truth dawns. If now 62 ♚xh5 ♞f6+!! 63 ♞xf6 g3 and the black pawn queens. For the moment, therefore, as a result of White's error on move 60, he cannot pluck Black's kingside pawns.

62	♚h4	♞f4
63	♞d2	♚a6
64	♞c4	e4
65	b5+	♚a7
66	♞e3	♚b6
67	♚g5	

The saving grace. White's knight manoeuvre, having prodded the black e-pawn from e5–e4,

has undermined the protection of the black knight. Therefore, White still has time, but only just, to eliminate the black kingside pawns.

67	...	♞e2
68	♚xh5	g3
69	♚g5	♚xb5
70	♚f5	♞c3
71	♚f4	

Black cannot now repeat the knight fork trap we saw before since 71 ... ♞d5+ 72 ♚xe4 ♞xe3 72 ♚xe3 g2 74 ♚f2 is a draw.

| 71 | ... | ♚c5 |
| 72 | ♚e5 | ♚b4 |

There is really nothing else for Black to do.

73	♚f4	g2
74	♞xg2	♚c4
	Draw agreed	

A Battle Royal in one sense, but a Battle of errors in another. Very instructive study material for those plotting to beat their own computer.

REBEL–FIDELITY
1st Computer Olympiad, 1989

1	d4	f5
2	♞c3	♞f6
3	♝g5	d5
4	♞f3	♞bd7
5	e3	c6
6	♝d3	♛b6
7	♜b1	e6
8	0–0	♝d6

9	♘e2	c5
10	c4	♘e4
11	b4!!	

It is surprising that FIDELITY, which the previous day had conducted a difficult endgame of knights and passed pawns, should so utterly have overlooked the devastating effects of 11 b4. After that, Black might as well have given up.

11	...	♛c7
12	bxc5	♘xg5
13	♘xg5	♗xh2+
14	♚h1	♘f6
15	g3	♘g4
16	cxd5	exd5

17	♘f4	a6
18	♘fe6	♗xe6
19	♘xe6	♛d7
20	♗xf5	♘f6
21	♚xh2	g6
22	♗h3	♖b8
23	♛f3	♛e7
24	c6	b5
25	♘c7+	♚f7
26	♘xd5	♛d6
27	e4	♖he8
28	♖fc1	♖xe4
29	♘xf6	♛xf6
30	♛xe4	♖e8
31	♛xe8+	♚xe8
32	c7	♚f7
33	c8(♛)	♚g7
34	♖c7+	♚h6
35	f4	♛g7
36	g4	♛xc7
37	♛xc7	g5
38	♛f7	gxf4
39	♛f6+	mate

The authors now wish the readers luck in defeating their own machines!

10 Conclusion

What can we learn from the games that we have just analysed? As machines improve the answer must be that we have to continue to study their games and we must seek to understand their methods of play. A natural symbiosis suggests itself. It seems obvious that if computers begin to beat the very best human players then it will be possible to raise the standard of human play by working with computers in an attempt to grasp how they achieve their improved results. By sharpening the human mind the struggle of man versus machine will metamorphose into a totally different proposition. Just as man's collaboration with the internal combustion engine has led to increased records in speed, so in the long term the advent of computers will prove beneficial in the development of human chess.

The alternative is less appetizing. If we ignore the advances in computer chess and do not regard their improvement as a spur, but rather as a large and threatening shadow, the less able Grandmasters (not to mention lesser players) will rapidly find that the machines are overtaking them. In a couple of decades computers, if left solely to their own devices, may well by playing for the World Championship itself. Like the last emperor of China it will not be an enviable epitaph to be known as the last human chess champion of the world.

Do Computers Think Like People?

The idea of automating human thought processes dates back at least two hundred years and has fascinated mankind ever since. It was in the late 18th century in Austria that Baron Wolfgang von Kempelen, Aulic Councillor to the Royal Court of Vienna, built the "Automaton" that could play a brilliant game of chess. Represented by a life-sized figure of a Turk seated on a box, the Automaton amazed spectators and reputedly caused one courtier to faint. There was, of course, a man hidden inside the box, but Kempelen's elaborate box was not futile — it sowed the seed of "thinking" machines.

A few decades after von Kempelen, the English mathematician and engineer Charles Babbage designed his "analytical engine" which, alas, was not completed. As early as the 1840s Babbage considered it feasible to make such a device play chess. In "The Life of a Philosopher" he wrote:

> After much consideration I selected for my test the contrivance of a machine that should be able to play a game of purely intellectual skill successfully; such as tit-tat-to [noughts and crosses — DL], drafts, chess, etc.

What Babbage could only dream about became a reality with the advent of the electronic computer just over a century later. The first program to play chess was written for an IBM 704 computer in 1957 but, not surprisingly, it played a very weak game. Ten years later a program written at MIT was strong enough to play in local amateur tournaments, and by 1970 there was sufficient interest in computer chess to hold regular tournaments in which all of the contestants were computer programs. Spurred on by the desire to win these tournaments, chess programmers made steady progress during the 1970s and 1980s. As we enter the 1990s the question being asked is no longer "Can a program defeat a future World Champion?", but "When will a program beat Kasparov?". An electronic chess "Grandmaster", DEEP THOUGHT, is already with us, sitting on a printed circuit board small enough to fit inside a briefcase.

Many argue that computers, or more precisely computer programs, cannot think, that they cannot be intelligent. I do not intend to address this philosophical question here, beyond making the point that "everyone knows" that one needs to be intelligent to play good chess. DEEP THOUGHT has beaten Grandmasters, ergo it must be intelligent.

Relying on the premise that computer programs do think, let us now consider whether games playing programs think in an analogous way to humans. In chess, at least, the answer appears to be yes and no.

The programming structure which enables a program to play chess and several other games is called a "tree". The program's task is to decide on a move from a given position, and it represents that position as the "root" of the tree. Each of the possible moves from a position is represented by a "branch" of the tree and at the other end of a branch is the new position.

Growing a tree to represent the myriad possibilities on the chessboard is a straightforward task, accomplished by a module in the program called the "legal move generator". What is much more difficult for a program is accurately evaluating the positions that arise in the tree. Without a reasonably sensible "evaluation function" a program could look a long way ahead but have little or no understanding of what it was looking at.

Clearly some chess knowledge is needed in the evaluation function but representing such knowledge in purely numeric terms is far from simple. With little knowledge at its disposal, an evaluation function will provide only a crude, often erroneous distinction between good positions and bad ones. With a lot more chess knowledge the evaluation function becomes much more accurate, and will sometimes be able to pick the best move in a position without using a look-ahead. But one of the problems facing chess programmers is that evaluation functions with more knowledge require more time to compute, reducing the depth of look-ahead that can be achieved within the allotted time per move. A search which thereby becomes too shallow can lead a program to make tactical oversights, unnecessarily losing material or succumbing to checkmate.

Evaluation functions in games playing programs are also employed to determine which moves a program should examine, making selectivity possible. With an average of 37 moves in a chess position, it is easy to comprehend that the problem of looking ahead to a significant depth can be immense. After only one move by each side there are more than 1,000 positions to evaluate. After two moves by each side the number rises to over 1 million. DEEP THOUGHT, by using some clever programming tricks, looks at everything at least five moves ahead by each side, and it examines the tactical variations which it considers most interesting to a depth of 10, 15 or even more moves by each side. In contrast to these telephone numbers a strong human player will typically evaluate only 50–150 positions during a 3 minute analysis. Herein lies the big difference in thinking between human Grandmaster and computer Grandmaster — the human knows which moves to select for examination. His evaluation function is sufficiently knowledgeable.

It is possible to summarize the difference in thinking between DEEP

THOUGHT and Gary Kasparov thus. The computer performs the task of evaluation fairly competently but not brilliantly, though it does so millions of times whenever called upon to decide on its move. In attempting to emulate and surpass human Grandmasters it performs the task of evaluation less intelligently, in the chess sense, but it does so much more often. Kasparov's evaluation function is fine-tuned to the point of perfection, but he needs to apply it less than once per second. He uses his accurate evaluative skill to select those moves which deserve to be considered, and to prune out the dross. His highly selective search enables Kasparov to keep the size of his own game tree to within manageable proportions.

Because chess programmers have not yet been able to encapsulate all human chess knowledge in numeric evaluation techniques, the art of chess programming has largely relied on ever faster hardware. DEEP THOUGHT uses a microchip designed specifically and only to play chess and which performs the tasks of move generation and position evaluation at amazing speeds. A debate has long raged between two schools of chess programmers: which of "selective search" and "brute force" should be the more successful strategy? At the moment the brute force school is winning, so one needs to ask the question "Will mere brute force alone be enough to defeat Kasparov?" There are those, including DEEP THOUGHT's designers, who believe that existing evaluation techniques, together with an extra 2 moves of look-ahead for each side, will be sufficient to create an electronic monster strong enough to challenge the human World Champion. Others, notably the stronger chess players within the computer chess fraternity, believe that greater selectivity (i.e. more embedded chess knowledge) will be required.

Amongst the thinking games that have been programmed, chess has been witness to some of the greatest successes. It is estimated that some 10,000 people have written chess programs. More than 20 books, dozens of university theses and hundreds of academic papers have appeared on the subject. This information has been available for those who have programmed other thinking games, with the result that human champions have been vanquished in activities other than chess, but in most cases the "thought processes" of the programs have been very different from those of human players.

Appendix: Buying a Chess Computer

In this chapter we shall describe most of the features that can be found in commercially available chess computers and in chess programs that are available for personal computers. The reader who is trying to decide which dedicated chess computer or which personal computer program to buy, will find it useful to think about these features and to decide which ones, for him or her, are the most important. He/she can then devise his or her own evaluation function, assigning a weighting to each of those features which he/she considers desirable, and by using this evaluation function he/she can compare the various products on the market and decide which is the most suitable for his/her individual requirements.

Input and Output

There are various ways in which it is possible to enter moves into a computerized chess player, and in which the electronic opponent can indicate its moves to the user. In this section we consider the various options.

Co-ordinate Entry

The very first chess computers on the market all required the user to enter his moves by keying them into the computer using a form of algebraic chess notation. It is sufficient for a computer to know the location of the square from which the piece moves (the "from" square), and the square to which it moves (the "to" square), and so the user need only key in these two pairs of co-ordinates, and then press the ENTER key. Some users experienced difficulty with this concept at first, perhaps because they were not serious chess players and had never before encountered chess notation of any sort. Others, particularly those who lived in North America and Britain, were accustomed to descriptive notation and found it slightly annoying to have to change the habits of a lifetime and adopt algebraic notation. But any intelligent person can understand algebraic notation after no more than 5 minutes study, so any resistance to the use of chess notation was short lived, at least during the early days of chess computers.

The user would key in his moves on a keyboard that had eight keys specially for this purpose. Each of the eight keys has two functions, and the function depends on what stage has been reached in the move entry process. When the user is about to start entering his move, the keys allow him to enter any of the first eight letters of the alphabet, a–h. Once he has pressed one of these keys, the letter that he has indicated will normally appear on an electronic display so that it can be verified – the display will usually be either an LED (light emitting diode) display, which is most often red, or it might be an LCD (liquid crystal display) which usually appears in black and various shades of grey.

When the user has entered the letter part of the "from" square, the eight move entry keys change their function and now correspond to the numbers 1–8. The user then presses a key to enter the number part of the "from" square, and now the keys change function again so that the next keystroke will enter the letter part of the "to" square. Finally, after changing function again, the keys will allow the entry of the numerical part of the "to" square. When the user has entered his move, and the display shows E2E4 or whatever, he presses the ENTER key and the computer should now verify that the user's move is legal, before starting to compute its reply move. If the move is not legal the computer usually indicates this by showing four question marks in the display area, and possibly by producing an unpleasant tone (if it has a buzzer – see SOUND, page 98).

Co-ordinate entry of the user's moves is still used today (1991) by some chess programs, and there is nothing whatsoever wrong with this method. There are, however, some other methods of move entry which have gained popularity during the past few years.

Sensor Boards

Some computers use chess boards that have membrane keyboards beneath them. When a piece is pressed down on the centre of a square, it "makes" a switch in the membrane keyboard, which in turn indicates to the computer which square has been identified. So by pressing down with his piece, the user is entering both of the algebraic co-ordinates of the "from" square. (Some chess computers have a plug-in board and when the user picks up his piece he must first press it down on its present square.) When the user moves his piece to its new square, and presses down on the centre of this square with the piece, the computer registers the chosen "to" square and verifies the move for legality before starting to analyze its reply.

Sensor boards have an obvious advantage over co-ordinate entry devices – the user moves his piece in much the same manner as he does when playing chess against a human opponent. There is no need for the user to understand chess notation and so absolute beginners can actually learn chess by playing with a sensory chess computer.

There are different ways in which a sensor board computer can indicate its responses to the user. One method is to have a coloured light (LED) on each square of the chessboard, and for the computer to indicate the "from" square and the "to" square by switching on these LEDs. Perhaps the LED on the "from" square will flash on and off while the LED on the "to" square remains on all the time. Another approach is to have 16 LEDs located around two edges of the board, eight corresponding to the files of the chessboard (a–h) and eight corresponding to the ranks (1–8). When the computer wishes to indicate a square it does so by switching on the two LEDs corresponding to the rank and file of the square, and the user locates the square in question by finding the intersection of the two LEDs. This method is particularly appropriate for small chessboards where the individual squares might be too small to accommodate an LED without the square appearing crowded, and many of the very inexpensive chess computers on the market today employ this technique. One problem in using the 16 LEDs when the board is not small is that the user may find it difficult to locate certain squares which are far from the nearest LEDs. For example, if the LEDs are situated to the left of the a-file and below the 1st rank, then if the computer indicates the square h8 the user's eye must locate the intersection of the h-file LED and the 8th-rank LED, and the distance from these LEDs to the intersection may cause the user slight problems if the chessboard is not small. For this reason, one improvement is to use 32 LEDs instead of 16 and place them all round the board. The intersection of the rank and file LEDs will always be relatively near to the closest LEDs, which eliminates the minor problem mentioned earlier, and this method also has the advantage of allowing the user to continue to play with his chess computer if one of the LEDs goes wrong – it will still be possible to identify the squares indicated by the computer by referring to the remaining, working LED in that rank or file. We should emphasise, however, that LEDs are ultra reliable and it is extremely unlikely that even a single LED on your chess computer will fail during the lifetime of the product.

Magnetic Sensor Boards

A further improvement on the membrane board sensor technology described above, is to use a chess set with magnets in the base of each piece, and with magnetic sensitive switches beneath each square of the chessboard. The program knows whether or not a particular square of the board is occupied, by whether or not the corresponding switch has been activated by a magnet. Since the program knows which squares are occupied before a player begins to make his move, it can detect which piece the user wishes to move by noting which switch is next activated, and the square to which the piece is moved is the next one activated after that.

So far as I am aware the first person to design such a board was David Cahlander, of Control Data Corporation, who designed a board to connect to the Northwestern University programs (CHESS 4.0, CHESS 4.1, ... etc.) which run on CDC computers. The attraction of the magnetic sensory board is that the user is freed from the "onerous" task of pressing down the moving piece on the "from" square and the "to" square. One simply picks it up and puts it down, and if the software is well written one can even slide a piece across the board without the program getting confused by "seeing" the piece move to several different squares during the course of one move. This type of board is extremely pleasant to play with, and we would recommend the extra investment in a really well made wooden board for those who can afford it.

Magic Boards

Magnetic sensory boards do not have the ability to recognize which piece is on each occupied square of the board, they only know which squares are occupied and which are not. This information is sufficient to enable a program to work out what move is being made by the user, but it would be so much nicer if the program could recognize each piece, so that one could set up any position simply by placing the pieces on their squares, and the program would know what was where.

Ken Thompson, programmer of BELLE, built such a board in 1980. Each piece has a coil in the base, and by using resonance techniques the hardware was able to find out, in effect, how many turns of wire were on the coil situated above each square. The individual piece types each had their own individual number of turns, and so recognition of the pieces was an easy task.

Move Entry by Cursor Control

Chess programs that run on personal computers will often have a chessboard displayed on a television screen or monitor. The pieces will sometimes be moved by entering chess notation in the usual way, the "from" square and then the "to" square, on the computer keyboard. But an alternative method is to have a cursor on the screen, which starts life at the beginning of a move at a particular part of the screen, say the bottom left hand corner. The cursor is then moved, by means of a joystick or using direction keys on the computer keyboard, until it is situated on the "from" square. The user then presses an ENTER key on the computer keyboard, or the joystick button, to indicate to the computer that this is the piece which should be moved. The user then employs the same method to move the cursor to the "to" square, and once there he presses ENTER or pushes the joystick button again. This method has also been used with success in conjunction with an LCD chessboard, and since it requires no understanding of chess notation it is likely to remain popular.

Touch Sensitive LCDs

One idea which was much vaunted during late 1981 was that of touch sensitive LCD chessboard. This chessboard was approximately 3 inches square, and showed representations of each piece made from a number of LCD segments on each square of the board. By means of special technology the user was able to indicate the "from" square and "to" square of his moves simply by touching those squares on the LCD board with his finger, and the program would know which squares he was indicating. At least, that was the idea. It turned out that the technology was rather unreliable in a consumer environment, and the product containing this LCD was initially a failure. We see no reason why this technology cannot be made reliable in the future, but one other disadvantage exists with this method – repeated touching of the surface of the LCD makes it dirty, and dirt shows up rather badly on an LCD.

Robotic Movement

An idea which caught the imagination of the public as long ago as February 1979, is that of having a robot move the pieces for the computer. At that time one of us (David Levy) had been invited to play a demonstration game on German television against the Northwestern University program, and with the help of David Cahlander the program, playing on a computer in Minneapolis, was linked by satellite to an enormous robot arm located in the studio in Hamburg. In fact the arm was so big that a micro-switch was used to prevent it from stretching too far forward and hitting David on the head.

David sat in a soundproof glass booth, facing the Swedish built robot. Between David and the computer was the Cahlander magnetic chessboard. Whenever the program moved, the robot would return to its "control" position and then it infallibly picked up the program's piece and moved it to its new square. When the program made a capturing move the robot would first pick up David's piece, the one being captured, and deposit it in the box at the side of the board. Finally, when the game was drawn after some 10 hours play (which had been interrupted several times because of breakdowns in the satellite communications), the robot pushed forward its pincers to shake hands with David!

The popularity of the event can be judged from the fact that some 70,000 people wrote in to the television station to obtain copies of the game score together with annotations supplied by both players. Soon after that programme was screened, two companies started work on robot arms that were to be an integral part of commercially available chess computers. Both of these products were relatively expensive, and neither was a commercial success.

Later, one company launched a robotic chess computer which works in a different way. Instead of having an arm to move the pieces from above the board, the Milton-Bradley "Grandmaster" (called the Phantom in England) uses an electro-magnetic mechanism situated beneath the board, out of sight of the user. The electo-magnet moves along two axes and can therefore be placed below any part of the chessboard. When the electro-magnet is switched on it takes control of whichever piece is situated directly above it, since each piece has a magnet in its base. The piece is then slid across the board to its new square. Captured pieces are put on special locations at the side of the board, so that when a game is over the robot knows where all the pieces are and can set them up ready for the next game. If part of the board becomes crowded, or if a knight needs to move across an occupied square, the robot simply moves any obstructions out of the way, slides the piece to its new square, and then replaces the obstruction on their original locations. This is real magic, and the price of the magic is much more affordable than that of the robot arms. Another advantage of this particular approach is that because the mechanism is hidden from view, it is much less likely to be damaged by careless handling, whereas it is very easy for someone to accidentally knock a robot arm out of alignment.

Chess-specific Features

Legal Move Verification

It is by no means unknown for a chess computer to allow illegal moves by the user, or to make illegal moves itself. Fortunately this statement was far more significant during the early days of commercially available chess computers.

One of the aspects of move legality which has scope for some smart programming, is the recognition of an illegal or impossible move at an early stage of the move entry process. The way that legal move verification usually works is that when the user presses the ENTER key, or does whatever signifies completion of his move, the program then checks for legality and signifies if the user has tried to make an illegal move. It would be neater if the program could recognize illegal move tries at the earliest possible stage. For example in the initial position, if the user started off by keying in A1 (the square occupied by a white rook), the program should immediately give an illegal move warning because the piece located on A1 cannot move. Few programs have this level of sophistication in their legal move verification process, yet it is not difficult to program.

Pawn Promotion

Most chess programs nowadays allow the user to underpromote, that is to say, the user may choose to promote a pawn to a knight, rook or bishop. This is hardly ever needed (in an entire chess playing career David needed to underpromote only once), but it is a sensible feature to include in a chess program. It is not so important if the program itself cannot underpromote, but it is more important for the user to have some means of underpromoting even if it requires the use of the Set-Up or Enter-Position mode after making the pawn move.

Understanding Draws

There are various ways in which a game of chess can end in a draw, and the better and more expensive chess computers can usually cope with most or all of these situations. A program which can count can know quite easily whether or not 50 moves have passed since the last pawn move or the last capture, and it can declare a draw if and when this occurs. Detecting a draw by stalemate is also not difficult, and a program which recognizes stalemate in the game tree will have the ability to make stalemate considerations part of its look-ahead strategy. Probably the most difficult area is that of draws by threefold repetition, because in order for them to be detected properly the program must compare the current position with every position at 2-ply intervals back as far as the previous pawn move or capture. This may require storing more of the game record than the chess computer's memory will allow, but at the very least a chess computer costing more than (say) £80 ought to be able to detect draws where the repetition has occurred during the past 6-ply, i.e. back and forth and back and forth, and preferably somewhat further back than that. Otherwise the program is likely to allow a draw by repetition without realising that it is doing so.

It is useful for chess programs to be able to recognize when a game is drawn through lack of mating material. For example, if there are just the two kings remaining on the board, or if one side has king and bishop against king, it is nice for the computer to announce the draw. One chess computer, which sold extremely well during 1982, even went so far as to announce a draw if it remained with king, bishop and knight against king, since the program knew that it did not have the ability to force mate with that material configuration!

Offering Draws

Against a few select chess programs the user can offer a draw. This is usually done by making the draw offer at the same time as entering the user's move, paralleling the situation in a human v human game played under tournament rules, where one's draw offer should accompany one's move. The program then considers its reply move, and evaluates the resulting position, so that if the resulting position has a negative score (i.e. worse than a draw) the program will accept the offer. (Some programs have a "contempt factor" which requires them to refuse the draw offer unless they are behind by some fixed measure, say half a pawn.)

Playing Strength

After ensuring that your chess program understands the legal niceties of the game, the next most important feature to consider is almost certain to be its playing strength. If you are a beginner or a very weak player, and have no aspirations to become somewhat stronger, then all you need is a program which is capable of beating you on at least one of its playing levels. On the other hand, if you are interested in improving your play, you will want to buy the strongest program that your pocket allows. How can you find out which program is the strongest?

Nearly all chess computer manufacturers would have you believe that their programs are the strongest. If you see any advertising copy that makes claims of this kind, and then you buy the product and discover later that the claims are unfounded, you should complain vociferously. After all, chess is one of those few areas where it is possible to prove if A is stronger than B — simply play a match between the two. For a more worthwhile guide to the strength of a chess program we would recommend that you try to find out what computer chess tournaments the program has competed in and which it has won, and also find out whether the program has an official rating awarded by a national chess federation.

Openings Book

Most chess programs nowadays have their own openings book to ensure that the user can enjoy a variety of different openings and defences. The most useful information here is how many moves are in the openings book. It is possible to get a little variety if the answer is 100 or more, though you obviously cannot expect depth. If the number of book moves is anything between 150 and 500 then you can have quite a lot of variety, and some of the more important variations will probably go to a depth of 6 moves or more. If there are more than 500 moves most chess enthusiasts should be satisfied, and with 2,000 or more all but 1% of the world's chess players will be perfectly happy.

Hardware Features

Is it Modular?

As chess programs get stronger and stronger, many enthusiasts are anxious that their products can be upgraded whenever a new version of the program appears. This is possible if the chess computer is "modular" in some way, in other words, if the present program can be easily removed (by the user or the shop) and a new program put in its place. If you are concerned about playing strength you may also be concerned about modularity, so when you buy your chess computer ask not only whether it is modular, but whether the manufacturer has any other modular products on the market and if so, whether he had made available any new modules since the product was launched. It is all very well having a modular unit, but if no more modules are going to be produced by the manufacturer ...

Mains/Battery Operation

Some chess computers are only operated by battery. Others may only be operated from a mains power adaptor. Some can run off either. If your machine allows battery operation you should look in the advertising and on the packaging to see how long you can expect from the life of your batteries. The differences can be quite staggering. Some chess computers will run for only a few hours (anything from 2 to 12 would be considered quite normal). Others, which employ the lowest power

CMOS microchips, can have a battery life of anything up to a few hundred hours.

If a power adaptor is required (or is an option) your chess computer manufacturer will probably have ensured that the adaptor complies with all of your national safety regulations, but if the adaptor seems to get very hot when you have been playing for some time, have it examined for safety.

Power-Down Memory

Some chess computers use very low power memories so that you can switch to a special power-down mode in the middle of a game, and return to the game hours, days or even weeks later, when the computer will have retained the current board position. This feature is particularly useful when playing with a power adaptor, in case the adaptor is kicked or otherwise accidentally disconnected from the computer, when the position will be lost unless there is a low power memory-save feature. The chess computers that incorporate this feature usually allow sufficient storage for the computer to remember not only the position, but also the moves of the game (or at least the last few moves), and the status of castling rights.

LCD Chessboard

If you want to play chess without the need to carry a chess set with you, and if you do not like the small plug-in chess computers that are available at very low prices, an LCD chessboard is ideal for you. You may find with some LCD chessboard computers that the representation of the pieces is not to your taste, so before buying you should look at what is available. Just switch on for the start of a game and see whether you like the look of the pieces. The computer will almost certainly use a cursor method for move entry, and there are different ways of implementing such a cursor, so you should also try to make a few moves in the shop, before you buy, so that you can decide whether you are happy with the particular approach being used.

Chess Clocks

Serious chess players are interested in playing games where both sides have the same amount of thinking time at their disposal. For this reason some chess computers and some personal computer chess programs have a built in chess clock. The method of displaying the times usually requires some hardware, such as an LCD, and this is why I have included chess clocks in this section, though it is software which measures how much time has elapsed between moves.

It is useful, if you do have a chess clock, to be able to turn the clock on and off independently of whether a game is in progress. This is so that if you interrupt a game you can stop the clock and when you come back to the board you can start it.

Sound

Most chess computers have a buzzer, and ideally this can be switched on and off at will. The purpose of the buzzer is usually to act as an audible feedback when you key in a move or when you press down a piece on a membrane keyboard, and in this way the buzzer helps you to know that you have pressed the key properly. The other use of the buzzer is to warn you, with a sour tone, when you have tried to make an illegal move.

Printer

For the serious enthusiast it is nice to be able to print out the moves of a game as it is in progress, together with a diagram of the position on the chessboard whenever you wish. Or you may prefer to print out the whole of the move record at the end of the game.

Some chess computer manufacturers have allowed for this facility by including these features in their software and by supplying small printers which can be purchased as peripherals, to connect to the chess computer. Some of the chess programs available for personal computers also include software to allow the use of a printer. If you are particularly interested in the printer capability of a program, you should find out exactly what can be printed and when, and see how this compares with the corresponding features on rival products.

Speech

A few chess computers incorporate speech synthesis, so that the computer speaks the moves and announces check with an electronic voice. This is